American Chatterbox

TEACHER'S BOOK 4

A. WARD AND J.A. HOLDERNESS

OXFORD UNIVERSITY PRESS

Oxford University Press

200 Madison Avenue
New York, NY 10016 USA

Great Clarendon Street
Oxford OX2 6DP England

OXFORD and OXFORD AMERICAN ENGLISH are
trademarks of Oxford University Press.

ISBN 0-19-434603-X

Copyright © 1994 by Oxford University Press.

No unauthorized photocopying.

All rights reserved. No part of this publication may be
reproduced, stored in a retrieval system, or transmitted,
in any form or by any means, electronic, mechanical,
photocopying, recording, or otherwise, without the prior
permission of Oxford University Press.

This book is sold subject to the condition that it shall
not, by way of trade or otherwise, be lent, resold, hired
out, or otherwise circulated without the publisher's prior
consent in any form of binding or cover other than that in
which it is published and without a similar condition
including this condition being imposed on the subsequent
purchaser.

The publishers would like to thank Jennifer Bassett,
Hermione Leronymidis, and Lucy McCullagh for their
help in the preparation of Chatterbox Level 4.

Printing (last digit): 10 9 8 7 6 5 4 3

Printed in Hong Kong.

INTRODUCTION

General description of the series

American Chatterbox is a four-level course for children of elementary school age who are learning English for the first time. *American Chatterbox* Levels 1 and 2 cover the first year of study. Levels 3 and 4 cover the second year. There are fifteen units in each level. A unit contains material for three lessons of 50 minutes each with additional material for extra work in class and for homework.

The components at each level are a Student Book, a Workbook, a Teacher's Book, and a cassette.
The Student Book presents new words, grammar structures, and functions in imaginative and clear contexts. A continuing adventure story, featuring the children Ken, Kate, and Caroline; and a variety of songs, rhymes, and games are used to practice new language in an enjoyable way. The story, songs, and various other listening activities are recorded on the cassette.
The **Workbook** consolidates the language points of the Student Book with reading and writing exercises and puzzles, and can be used in class or for homework.
The **Teacher's Book** gives step-by-step lesson plans, answers, and extra ideas for classroom activities.

Aims

The three main aims of *American Chatterbox* are:
- to help students understand and use some basic structures of English grammar correctly in a variety of purposeful communicative activities.
- to help students develop confidence in listening, speaking, reading, and writing in English, using a good basic range of vocabulary.
- to make learning English an enjoyable and meaningful experience through an exciting story, songs, rhymes, games, and puzzles.

Scope and Sequence

The scope and sequence of *American Chatterbox* is based on graded structures and vocabulary. Language items have been chosen according to the criteria of frequency, usefulness, and simplicity, although some words are occasionally introduced which are specific to a particular story episode or topic. Each language item is recycled and reviewed regularly.

Closely linked to the structural scope and sequence is the scope and sequence of functions and topics, which covers areas of interest within the experience of children. Through interesting topics *American Chatterbox* systematically develops students' motivation and skills in listening, speaking, reading, and writing.

Characters in *American Chatterbox*

The story episodes revolve around the adventures of three children — Kate, Caroline, and Ken — Ken's dog, Barker, and Kate's Uncle John, who is a magician. In Book 3 Uncle John's old enemy, Spider Smith, steals Uncle John's magic book and tries to use magic to become rich. Uncle John and the children manage to spoil his plans and win a reward in the process. With the reward money, John and the children make a Time Machine, which can go forward into the future or backward into the past. Book 4 follows their travels as they try to find an ancient book of magic: the Book of Adabra.

How to use the Series Books

Each unit of the Student Book and the Workbook is four pages long. One unit provides work for a minimum of three 50-minute lessons.

Lesson One

Student Book: first page of the unit.

Workbook: first page of the unit.

The first page of the Student Book unit presents the main new structure and vocabulary for the unit, usually with an accompanying cassette section. The new language is then practiced in class through oral drills and through a question and answer activity, often introduced in the Student Book by Ken and Kate, shown as "talking heads." The talking heads give model questions and answers which students use to start talking about the pictures in the Student Book.

The first page of the Workbook unit contains follow-up reading and writing exercises to consolidate the new language.

Lesson Two

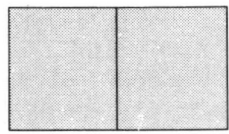

Student Book: second and third pages of the unit.

Workbook: second page of the unit.

The first part of this lesson is based on the adventure story which starts on the second page of every Student Book unit. Students listen to the Cassette and read the story in their books. They then role play the story in class. The second part of the lesson is based on the lower half of the third page of the Student Book unit. This page presents the secondary language point of the unit.

The second page of the Workbook follows up the story page with exercises to develop students' reading and writing skills.

Lesson Three

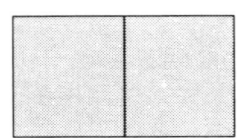

Student Book: fourth page of the unit.

Workbook: third and fourth pages of the unit.

The third lesson provides opportunities for students to extend their use of new language through a reading activity or a game or a song. The reading texts are usually based on topics loosely drawn from the story pages, which, while extending students' knowledge of the world, should be of inherent interest.

The corresponding pages of the Workbook (pages 3 and 4 of the unit) consolidate the language students have learned in that unit, usually ending with a puzzle.

Basic procedures — stages of the lesson

Review/Warm-up

In the warm-up at the start of each lesson students use language they already know, often in an activity they have done before: a song or a short game. The warm-up should last for no more than five minutes.

Presentation

New language is sometimes first presented to students with their Student Book closed, so that when they do open their books at the beginning of the unit some of the words and their meanings are already familiar, and interesting language practice can begin more quickly and easily.

Presenting new language with books closed.
New words and phrases are usually taught by showing real objects, by drawing simple pictures on the board, or by mime and gesture. Wherever possible, it is best to use real objects to present new words. In Books 3 and 4, students are expected to guess some words from context. Only use the students' first language to translate words when other methods of explanation are impossible.

Whenever a new word is introduced, make sure that students know how to pronounce it clearly. Use this procedure:
- Say the new word two or three times.
- Have students listen and repeat the new word, first all together and then individually.

Encourage students to compare new words or structures with those they already know in English and to explain for themselves rules of spelling and use.

Presenting new language with books open.
This method of presentation relies on the pictures on the Student Book page and often on the cassette recording that goes with it. There are three basic types of listening presentation which use the Student Book and the cassette.

   1. *Listen and repeat.* This procedure is used to present rhymes and other new language students can learn by heart.
   2. *Listen and point.* Have students listen to the tape and point to the appropriate object or person in the picture.
   3. *Listen and read.* This procedure is used to present the story page.

INTRODUCTION

Story presentation

Before presenting a new episode of the story, summarize what has happened in the story so far by discussing it with students in their first language. Ask them to tell you briefly what they remember about previous episodes.

Also before listening to the new story episode, pre-teach some of the new words that students will need to understand what happens. Use gesture and mime or board drawings to do this. Ask the focus questions given in the Teacher's Book notes and write them on the board so that students can refer to them while they are listening.
- Play the cassette section for the story episode right through once while students listen and read.
- Play the story again. Have students listen and look for answers to focus questions.
- After listening to the story, check the answers with students and go on to any further activities suggested in the notes.

Practice speaking and listening

Drills. The aim of speed drills is to help students learn the pronunciation and patterns of new language. They should be done at a rapid, lively pace.
- For new words: hold up or point to objects, pictures, etc. Have students name them in chorus, then individually. Go faster and faster.
- For structures: say a cue-word or phrase once or twice. Have students respond by giving a whole sentence, using the required structure. Again, keep up a rapid pace.

"Chain drills." Use the following procedure:
- Have one student make a statement to the next student, e.g., *Hello. My name's George. What's your name?* The next student replies, *Hello. My name's Maria,* and then turns to a third student and says, *What's your name?* Have students continue in this way around the class, each student in turn adding a new "link" to the chain.

Question and answer practice. The *Ask and answer* sections in the Student Book give opportunities for slightly less controlled practice based on the pictures on the Student Book page. A model of the questions and answers needed to talk about the pictures is presented by the "talking heads."
- Begin by asking the questions yourself and helping students to reply.
- Gradually get students to take over the questioning so that they are asking and answering each other, looking at the pictures for their answers.

Pair work. Question and answer practice leads naturally on to pair work, where students ask and answer each other in pairs. Go around checking students' pronunciation and understanding.

Teacher questions and "transfer." In some lessons more "open" and varied questions are suggested which can be used to ask students about what they can see in the pictures on the page or what they have read or heard. They can often also be developed to ask students about themselves, their own situation and experience — this *transfer* of question and answer practice to the students' own world makes the use of English obviously meaningful for them and is strongly recommended wherever possible.

Dialogue/Role play from the story. In Student Book 4 the story is presented in narrative form to expose students to the most common story-telling forms. However, the Teacher's notes give a version of the story in script form, so that students can role play the story, if they wish.
- Have students prepare the script by writing the names of the speakers in the appropriate places. This task provides a check of their understanding of the dialogue exchanges in the narrative of the Student Book.
- Go through the script with the whole class, using a group of students to demonstrate the dialogue.
- Have students in groups practice the dialogue.
- Have one of two groups role play the story, using their scripts. It is helpful to have props to represent objects which appear in the story, such as the Book of Adabra.

Reading and writing

As students' abilities in reading English develop, so too do the variety of topics and the length of the reading passages in *American Chatterbox*. The reading passages in *American Chatterbox 4* give information about places that the characters visit in the story (Australia, Japan, ancient Egypt), or about topics that come up from the story (inside a space shuttle, robots, the planets), or about topics of general interest to children (stamps, *The Guinness Book of Records*). Exploit these reading pages in the Student Book by using the following procedure:
- Before reading: pre-teach any new words that students won't be able to work out for themselves.

- While reading: ask students to read silently on their own or aloud in turn around the class, or else to work out passages together in pairs. Choose the approach which best suits a particular class and their mood in a particular lesson.
  Go around helping as necessary, but encourage students to develop the skill of guessing meanings of unknown words from their context or from clues in the pictures, and not to worry if they do not understand every word.
- After reading: check answers with the whole class, especially if a reading page has been completed for homework. Ask further questions as suggested in the Teacher's notes.

The story as a springboard for reading and writing. The second page of the Workbook follows up the story page with exercises to develop students' reading techniques and to start them on the path to writing short texts themselves. The story narrative also provides a model for short picture compositions that appear in Workbook 4 (e.g., Unit 4, Unit 10, Unit 14). These picture compositions use characters from the story in situations which are slightly different from the story narrative but which draw upon the same topic vocabulary. Have students write the story, using the pictures and the cue words given in the book as a guide.

Other writing exercises in the Workbook. Most writing practice, for consolidation of new grammar and vocabulary, takes place in the *American Chatterbox* Workbook. Exercises can be done either in class or for homework. Introduce Workbook exercises in the following way:
- Go over one or two sentences from any written exercise orally first to ensure that all students understand the aim of the exercise and what they have to do. If the exercise is done in class and not for homework, go around checking and helping with students' work.

Spelling. Practice in spelling takes place regularly through a variety of suggestions for extra word games in class and through word puzzles in the Workbook. Follow the suggestions for the individual exercises and games in lesson notes.
To teach the spelling of a new word, use this procedure:
- Have students look at the word, cover it up, try to write it from memory, then have them uncover the word and check the correct spelling. Have them repeat this procedure until they can spell the word correctly.

Extra activities. Many "Extra" activities suggested in the lesson plans in the Teacher's Book involve writing in a creative way.

Special procedures for specific activities

Songs and rhymes

The songs, rhymes, and chants in *American Chatterbox* have usually been specially written to focus on specific points of grammar or areas of vocabulary. They are intended as fun, lively ways of presenting and then practicing new language so that students can remember it more easily. There are also some traditional American songs. Use the following procedure:
- Play the cassette section. Have students first listen with books either open or closed, as you wish.
- Play the cassette once or twice more. Have students listen and sing along with the song or recite the rhyme, following the words in their books.
- Encourage students to learn the songs and rhymes by heart for homework. Use them frequently for lesson "warm-ups" or endings, as suggested.

Games

In games students are able to practice using their English in the context of meaningful speaking and listening activities in which they can participate unself-consciously. A variety of easy-to-manage games are used in Level 4 of *American Chatterbox*.

Class or Team games in *American Chatterbox* include:
  Guessing games: "Guess the Dream" (Unit 1, Lesson 1), "Guess the Object" (Unit 2, Lesson 1).
  Word games: Word jumbles (Unit 12, Lesson 3),
  Listening games: the "Please and Thank You" game (Unit 3, Lesson 1).
  Discrimination games: "Which One Is Different?" (Unit 2, Lesson 2).
  Quizzes: "Robot Quiz" (Unit 3, Lesson 3).

Games for pairs in *American Chatterbox* include:
  Guessing games: "A guessing game: Who's in your family?" (Unit 5, Lesson 3).
  Reading games: see "A game: Cowboys and Indians" (Unit 7, Lesson 3).

INTRODUCTION

Games for individuals in *American Chatterbox* include:
Vocabulary games: Mimes/Charades (Unit 3, Lesson 1), "Bingo!" (Unit 13, Lesson 2).
Word puzzles: crossword puzzles, word search squares, letter chains, etc., in the Workbook.

Before starting to play a class or team game, the following procedures are recommended:

1. Name teams. Divide the class into teams. Give each team an English name, e.g., the Lions and the Monkeys. Vary the team names lesson by lesson to practice new words. Write team names on the board for scoring during games.

2. Choose players. Use a "choosing rhyme" such as the following, to add suspense and student involvement to the process of picking players for class or team games:

*Eeny, Meeny, Miney, Mo,
Choose a person; off we GO!*

The student chosen is the one you are pointing to on the word GO! Always get students to chant with you.

Dictations

Story-line dictations. These can be based on small pieces of text from recent story episodes. Similar dictations can be planned into any lesson, as necessary.
- Read out each section of the dictation twice. Have students listen and write.
- Have them try to fill in missing words from memory by saying the whole sentence to themselves.
- Alternatively, students can work together in pairs, agreeing on missing words, their spellings, etc.
- Have students check their own dictation by looking back at the relevant section of the story.

Picture (Picasso) dictations. These can be represented to students as "drawing games":
- Have students listen and draw in response to simple instructions. Give each instruction two or three times at near-normal speed and rhythm.
- Go over the "dictation" by getting students to listen again and take turns drawing on the board.

Tests

The *American Chatterbox* Tests, at the end of this Teacher's Book, provide a simple test of reading and writing skills for students to do after every fifth unit of the course. When giving a test from the book use the following procedure:
- Check that all students understand what they have to do. Go over the instructions and the example given for each section of the test and demonstrate what they should do.
- Have students complete the test exercises one by one.

Extra test suggestions are also given at the end of the Teacher's Book notes for Units 5, 10, and 15.

Use the students' results to determine where further teaching and further practice may be necessary for the whole class or for individuals. Evaluation of students' skills in speaking and listening should be done on the basis of their regular participation in class, but some suggestions for testing oral skills are included in the extra test ideas.

Scope and Sequence Chart

Unit	(Student Book page)	Language items	Functions	Topic
1	(page 1)	Review: Past simple. *Dream about...* Nationality adjectives.	Talking about dreams. Talking about nationality.	Stamps
2	(page 5)	*made of glass/plastic/wood...* Review: *Why?... Because...*	Talking about materials. Expressing difference.	A space shuttle
3	(page 9)	*must/must not + before/after/when ...* Review: *can/can't*.	Talking about rules. Insisting. Talking about ability.	Robots
4	(page 13)	Comparatives: adjective + *er*: small, smaller. Comparatives: *More* + adjective.	Comparing.	The planets
5	(page 17)	Jobs. Review: Present simple.	Talking about people's jobs, where they work, and what they do.	Jobs
6	(page 21)	Superlatives: *the* + adjective + *est*: the biggest. Superlatives: *the most* + adjective.	Comparing height, size, and ability. Talking about measurement.	*The Guinness Book of Records*
7	(page 25)	Review: Past simple and Future *(going to)*. *Last Friday & Next Friday. Last Friday/this week.* Review: Present continuous.	Talking about past actions and future plans. Using a diary.	Cowboys and Indians
8	(page 29)	*Would you like ...? Yes, please./No, thank you. I'd like ...*	Offering politely. Accepting and refusing politely. Expressing desire or preference.	Hollywood

Scope and Sequence Chart *continued*

Unit	(Student Book page)	Language items	Functions	Topic
9	(page 33)	Future: *Will you ...?* *Yes, I will./No, I won't.* *Maybe I'll ...* *He'll ...*	Talking about predictions and unplanned future actions. Making decisions. Talking about future intentions.	Australia
10	(page 37)	*Looks like, sounds like ...* Regular and irregular plurals	Describing one object by comparison with another.	Animals
11	(page 41)	*How much ...?* *I'll buy ...*	Talking about money and prices. Talking about future intentions.	Japan
12	(page 45)	Conjunction: *so ...* Review: *somebody, anybody, nobody, everybody.*	Talking about cause and effect. Talking about the weather. Retelling a story.	Ancient Egypt
13	(page 49)	Review: Past simple. *By plane, train,* etc. Review: Verbs.	Talking about past travel.	Ancient writing
14	(page 53)	Review: Directions. *Turn right/turn left.* *North, south, east, west.* Review: Past simple. *Afraid of ...*	Following and giving directions. Talking about fears.	Adventure story
15	(page 57)	Review.		

UNIT 1

Lesson One

Language focus
Review: Past simple.
Talking about dreams: *What do you dream about?*

New words
dream (verb)   *dreamed* (past tense)   *dream* (noun)

Review/Warm-up

1. Introduce yourself to any new students. Say: *Hello, I'm [Miss/Mrs./Mr. . . .]* and ask their names. Get students you already know to introduce themselves to new students in the same way.

2. Game: "Where did you go yesterday?" Say: *I went to the park yesterday. Where did you go yesterday, [Maria]?* The student should name a place, though in this case it doesn't have to be a true answer: *[Teacher's name] went to the park and I went to the zoo. Where did you go yesterday, [George]?* The game continues until all the students have had a turn. When a student forgets the correct sequence, he or she is out.

Presentation (STUDENT BOOK p.1 CS1*)

3. Dreams. Books closed. Before listening: Pre-teach *dream*. Say: *I went to bed at [time]. I slept. I dreamed last night. I dreamed about [a rabbit]. Did you dream [George]? Did you dream about a rabbit? What did you dream about?* Write *dream* on the board. Write the question and answer on the board: *What did you dream about? I dreamed about. . . .* Have students read the question and answer out loud.
- Books open. Help students to identify the characters in the story: Uncle John, Kate, Ken, Caroline, and Barker. Ask: *What are they doing? (They're sleeping, they're dreaming.) Where are they? (They're in the Time Machine.)* Say: *Point to the dinosaur/Spider Smith/Uncle John's magic book.*

4. Play CS1. Have students listen.
- Play CS1 again. Have students listen and point.

*CS1 refers to the cassette section number on the tape.

Tapescript

Voice 1: Listen and point.
Voice 2: Uncle John dreamed about Spider Smith. In the dream, Spider Smith wanted to steal a magic green stone from the museum, but Uncle John stopped him. He said a spell, "9, 3, 6 . . . SHAZAM!" and he changed Spider into a frog. He put Spider into a bag and telephoned the police.
Ken dreamed about the Time Machine. In Ken's dream, he and Kate and Caroline helped Uncle John make the Time Machine. When it was ready, Uncle John went inside with Barker. Caroline pressed a button. The Time Machine started to disappear. They were very worried and Caroline started to cry. But it was all right because Uncle John came back.
Caroline dreamed about their visit to the zoo. In Caroline's dream, the children and Uncle John went to see Coco, and Uncle John gave Coco some magic bananas. But suddenly an elephant picked up Uncle John. Uncle John didn't see the man on the elephant. It was Spider Smith! He stole Uncle John's magic book.
Kate dreamed about the dinosaur. In Kate's dream, Spider Smith changed some dinosaur bones into a real dinosaur. The dinosaur was very dangerous: it knocked down buildings and ate trees. The children and Uncle John followed the dinosaur to the park. Then Uncle John made a magic spell and changed the dinosaur back into bones again. Then they took it back to the museum.
Barker dreamed about Caroline's cat, Tiger. In *his* dream he chased Tiger up a tree. Barker was very happy because he likes to chase cats.

5. Practice questions and answers in the past tense. Ask: *Who dreamed about Spider Smith? Who dreamed about the dinosaur? What did Caroline dream about? What did Barker dream about? Where was the elephant? What did the dinosaur eat? What did Uncle John give Coco?*, etc.

Practice (STUDENT BOOK p.1)

6. Ask and answer: Read aloud the example question: *What do you dream about?* Have students make up an answer, using the pictures on p. 1 as a guide: (*I dream about monsters*, etc.)
- Pair work: Have students ask and answer using all the pictures on SB p. 1.

7. Transfer: Have students, in pairs or groups, ask and answer about their own dreams: *What do you dream about? (I dream about . . .).*
- Go around the class and help students with vocabulary where necessary.
- Write on the board: *I often dream about . . .* Make a list of some of the things that students in the class

UNIT 1

dream about. Then write on the board: *Do you dream about . . . ?* Have students in pairs of groups ask and answer questions about the items on the list.

Reading and writing (WORKBOOK p.1)

8. **Activity** ① Have students read the sentences and answer the questions.

Answers 1. Kate 2. Spider Smith 3. Ken 4. Caroline 5. Uncle John 6. Caroline

9. **Activity** ② Have students unscramble the words to find out what the characters are dreaming about. Tell students to make sentences.

Answers
Caroline is dreaming about the beach.
Kate is dreaming about monsters.
Uncle John is dreaming about chocolate.
Ken is dreaming about football.
Spider is dreaming about magic.
Barker is dreaming about bones.

Ending the lesson

10. (Extra) Dictation: *Uncle John gave Coco some magic bananas./Coco ate the bananas./An elephant picked up Uncle John./Spider Smith was on the elephant./He stole Uncle John's magic book.*

    • Write the title of the dictation, *Caroline's dream,* on the board.

    • Read through the dictation passage once out loud, have students listen only. Read again slowly, while students write. Read again for checking.

11. Game: "Guess the Dream." Tell students: *Last night I dreamed about something beginning with T. What did I dream about?* Have students take turns to asking: *Did you dream about [a telephone]?* (No, I didn't.) *Did you dream about [a tiger]?* (No I didn't.) *Did you dream about [a Time Machine]?* (Yes, I did.) The student who guesses correctly gets the next turn.

Be prepared!

Make "tickets" of the countries on SB p. 3 for the activity at the end of Lesson Two.

Lesson Two

Language focus
Nationality adjectives.

New words
Mars Australia Brazilian Canadian Chinese Greek Japanese Spanish robot

Review/Warm-up

1. Review SB p.1. Ask about the characters in the story: *What did Uncle John dram about? What did Kate dream about? What did Ken dream about? What did Caroline dream about? What did Barker dream about?*
   • Ask about students in the class: *What did you dream about?*

2. Game: "Guess the Dream": *Last night I dreamed about something beginning with . . .*

Story presentation (STUDENT BOOK pp.2–3, CS2)

3. *Forward to the future!* Review the story so far by referring to p.1: Ask: *Where are Uncle John and the children?* (in the Time Machine) *Who made the Time Machine?* (Uncle John).
   • Pre-teach new word: *Mars* by translation. Then ask: *Can you go to Mars? Can Uncle John go to Mars in his Time Machine?* Pre-teach *robot* by asking students to describe Zoko. Then say: *Zoko is a robot.*
   • Books open. Before listening: Ask: *Where are Uncle John and the children?* (in the Time Machine) *Can you see any robots?* (yes) *What's the date on the calendar in picture 1?* (2000) *Who has a crystal ball?* (Uncle John).
   • Write focus questions on the board:
     a. Why are they going to Mars? (Because they want to find the Book of Adabra.)
     b. Are they going into the past or the future? (the future)
     c. When do they stop? (2060)
     d. Where do they stop? (Mars)
   • Play CS2. Have students listen and read.
   • Play CS2 again. Have them listen and answer the questions on the board.

Story practice

4. Ask further questions about the story: *Where did Caroline see robots?* (in the crystal ball). *What did Uncle John see in his crystal ball?* (the Book of Adabra). *Where's the Book of Adabra now?* (on Mars). *What are they going to do next?* (find the Book of Adabra).

5. Dialogue: Give students copies of the dialogue from the story. Ask them, working in groups, to find out who is speaking by referring to the story. Then have them write down the names of the speakers on the script.

_____: Look at Barker! He's upside down and he's chasing his bone.*

_____: We're flying through space and we're going to Mars.

_____: Why are we going to Mars?

_____: Well, yesterday I looked in my crystal ball and I saw the book. Do you remember? I wanted to find a book of magic spells ... the Book of Adabra. Somebody lost the book a long time ago, but it is now on Mars. Look at the ball ...

_____: Yes, I can see the book ... and wow! I can see robots too!

_____: Well, we ARE going into the future!

_____: Yippee! Are we going to meet robots? Can they talk?

_____: Can they talk in English?

_____: Look at the calendar! It's 2050!

_____: We really are in the future now, Uncle John.

_____: Oops! What is it?

_____: We're stopping. It's 2060 ... and we're on Mars ... Yes, that's right.

_____: Ooh! Look at that city!

_____: Come on. Let's go and find the Book of Adabra.

- Check students' answers with the whole class. Ask them to tell you which words have been left out when making the story into a dialogue. Discuss the meaning of the quotation marks (they show the words that are actually spoken) and the purpose of, for instance, *she said* (to indicate who was speaking).
- Have one or two groups act out the dialogue, using their scripts. Give them something to represent the crystal ball and the Time Machine calendar. Encourage students to put in appropriate actions, for example, to laugh and point in the right places.

6. Summary completion: Write on the board: *Uncle John and the children flew through ... to Mars. They wanted to find ... They are going to meet ... They stopped in ... at a ... on Mars.* Have students come to the board and write in the missing words.

*You may photocopy this material for classroom use.

Presentation (STUDENT BOOK p.3, CS3)

7. *Children around the world.* Books open. Say: *Show me [Canada] on the map.* Have students point. Identify the other countries (Brazil, Spain, Egypt, Greece, Australia, China, Japan) in the same way.
- Play CS3. Tell students that the class is going to go around the world to see all these children from the different countries as they are mentioned on the tape.

Tapescript

Voice 1: Listen and point to the children in the right countries..
Voice 2: We're going to go around the world in a Time Machine. First we're going to go to Brazil to visit some Brazilian children.
Then we're going to go to Canada to visit some Canadian children.
After that, we're going to go to Japan to visit some Japanese children.
Then we're going to go to China to visit some Chinese children.
After that, we're going to go to Egypt to visit some Egyptian children.
Then we're going to go to Greece to visit some Greek children.
And after Greece, we're going to go to Spain to visit some Spanish children.
Then after that, we're going to go to Australia to visit some Australian children.

8. Have students read out loud the names of the countries and the nationalities. Make sure they can read and pronounce all the words. Say the name of a country: *Brazil*, and get students to respond: *Brazilian*. Continue until students can respond fairly quickly.

Practice (STUDENT BOOK p.3)

9. Ask further questions about the trip around the world: *Where are we going to go first? (Brazil) Who are we going to visit? (some Brazilian children)*, etc. Include the time markers *(then, after that,* etc.) in the questions.

Reading and writing (WORKBOOK p.2)

10. Activity ③ Have students read the story in their Student Book again and circle the correct answer.

Answers 1. right 2. right 3. wrong 4. wrong 5. right

11. Activity ④ Have students match the pictures and then write sentences.

UNIT 1

Answers
1. Barker can see some steak.
2. Kate can see a calendar.
3. Caroline can see some robots.
4. Ken can see a skateboard.
5. Uncle John can see some chocolate cake.

Ending the lesson

12. (Extra) Group work: Give each group some "tickets" on pieces of paper, for the countries mentioned on SB p. 3. Have students take turns picking up a ticket, and telling the group: *I'm going to go to [Japan] to visit some [Japanese] children.*

Lesson Three

Language focus
Review: Present simple.

New words
album   collect   most   (=the majority of)   place   stamp (noun)   wild   Britain   French   Kenyan   British   Russian

Review/Warm-up

1. Ask: *Where do Chinese children live? (in China).* Review all the other nationalities in the same way.
- Ask students to spell the nationalities learned so far. Divide the class into two teams. Each team sends a student to the board. Say the name of a country. The first student to write the nationality, spelled correctly, wins a point for his or her team.

Reading (STUDENT BOOK p.4, CS4)

2. *Stamps.* Before reading: Pre-teach new words *stamp, collect, album.* Show students some stamps, or point to the pictures on SB p. 4. Say: *These are stamps.* Ask: *Do you have any stamps? You collect stamps. Do you collect stamps, [George]? Where do you keep your stamps? You keep them in a stamp album.* Write the new words on the board.
- Books open. Pre-teach new nationalities: *French, Kenyan, British, Russian* by writing the countries on the board: *France, Kenya, Britain, Russia,* then asking students to find the nationalities among the captions for the stamps. Write the nationalities on the board next to the names of the countries.

3. Write focus questions on the board:
a. Where do Helen and Jane keep their stamps? (in stamp albums)
b. Who collects stamps with pictures of flowers on them? (Helen)
c. What do British stamps always show? (a picture of Queen Elizabeth)
d. Which stamp shows a park for wild animals? (the stamp from Kenya)
- Have students read silently. Have them answer the questions. Ask further questions: *What kind of stamps does Jane collect? (Stamps with pictures of animals on them) Do most stamps show the name of the country they come from? (yes) What does the stamp from America show? (a picture of a famous man: Martin Luther King, the black rights activist) Which stamp do you like?*

Answers
1. Jane wants the Australian stamp, the Kenyan stamp, and the Spanish stamp. ("Animals" can be taken to include birds and fish.)
2. Helen wants the British stamp and the Chinese stamp.

4. After reading: Books open. Say: *Point to the Japanese stamp,* etc. Have students point to the stamps as you name them.
- Play CS4. Have students listen and point.

Tapescript

Voice 1: Listen and point to the right stamps.
Voice 2: This is a Japanese stamp. It shows a Japanese woman in a red and blue dress. She's playing with a ball.
Look at this Spanish stamp. There's a picture of a blue bird and a snake on it. It's strange but very interesting.
Here's a Kenyan stamp with some wild animals on it. Behind the elephant there's a big tree. Can you see the tree house at the top?
Look at the Australian stamp. It shows a blue, yellow and green fish. The fish is swimming in the sea. Isn't it beautiful?
The Canadian stamp shows four boats. There are three small boats and one big boat.

5. Ask further questions about the stamps: *Which stamp shows some beautiful fish? (the Australian stamp) Which stamp shows a woman in a red dress? (the Japanese stamp) Which stamp has a picture of a bird and a snake on it? (the Spanish stamp),* etc.

Reading and writing (WORKBOOK pp.3–4)

6. WB p.3 **Activity** ⑤ Have students punctuate the sentences.

Answers "Why are we going to Mars?" asked Ken. "Well," Uncle John said. "Yesterday I looked in my crystal ball . . . and I saw a robot magician." "Did he have a magic wand?" asked Kate. "No," laughed Uncle John, "but his tricks were very good."

7. **Activity** ⑥ Have students read and match the dates and the calendars.

Answers 1. e 2. c 3. b 4. f 5. d 6. a

8. WB p.4 **Activity** ⑦ Have students complete the crossword puzzle.

Answers

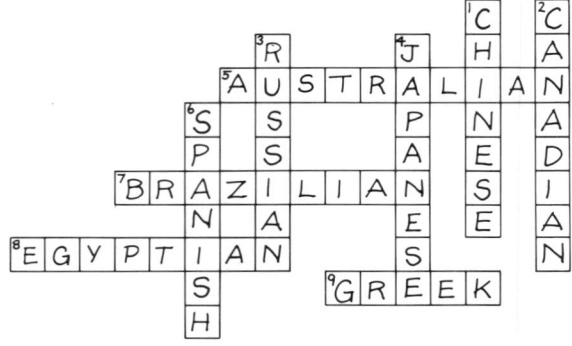

Ending the lesson

9. (Extra) Dictation: Dictate the first paragraph of the reading passage *Stamps* on SB p.4.
   • Read through the dictation passage once out loud, directing students to listen only. Read again slowly, while students write. Read again for checking.

10. (Extra) Project: Ask students to bring interesting stamps to class, to make a wall display.
    • Help students to write a caption for each stamp, for example: *This is a stamp from [Japan]. It shows ...*

UNIT 2

Lesson One

Language focus
Talking about materials: *It's made of glass/plastic/wood.*

New words
glass   made of   metal   plastic

Review/Warm-up

1. Revise nationalities. Say: *I've got a stamp from Russia.* Have students respond: *It's a Russian stamp,* etc.

Presentation (STUDENT BOOK p.5)

2. Pre-teach *made of, glass, plastic,* and *metal.* Touch the window. Say: *This is glass.* Touch the window frame and say: *And this is wood/metal.* Say: *The window is made of glass.* Do the same with other objects around the class. Write on the board: *glass, metal, plastic, wood, paper.* Then tell students: *[George], touch something made of glass. [Maria] touch something made of metal,* etc.

3. *What's it made of?* Books open. Look and say: Read the sentences with the whole class.
• Ask questions about the pictures: *What's made of plastic? (the comb) What's made of paper? (the newspaper),* etc.

Practice (STUDENT BOOK p.5, CS5)

4. Listen and point: Practice the sample question with the whole class. *What's this bowl made of?* Ask students to identify the objects in the picture: *Point to the shoe. Point to the vase,* etc.
• Play CS5. Have students listen and point.

Tapescript

Voice 1:   Listen and point.
Voice 2:   What's this bowl made of?
Voice 3:   It's made of glass.
Voice 2:   What's this shoe made of?
Voice 3:   It's made of wood.
Voice 2:   What's *this* bowl made of?
Voice 3:   It's made of metal.
Voice 2:   What's this knife made of?
Voice 3:   It's made of metal.

UNIT 2

Voice 2: What's this bird made of?
Voice 3: It's made of paper.
Voice 2: What's this ruler made of?
Voice 3: It's made of plastic.

Answers   8, 10, 4, 20, 9, 14

- Practice further questions about the pictures with the whole class. Write on the board: *What's this ... made of? It's made of ...* and *What are these ... made of? They are made of ...* Ask questions about the plural items (flowers, marbles).
- Pair work: Have students take turns asking and answering in the same way.

5. Ask and answer with the whole class: *What's the baseball bat made of?* (wood) *What's the dinosaur made of?* (plastic) *What are the white and red flowers made of?* (plastic) *What's the blue box made of?* (metal), etc.

Reading and writing (WORKBOOK p.5)

6. **Activity 1** Ask questions about the pictures: *What are these?* (bottles) *What are they made of?* (glass). *What's this?* (a box) *What's it made of?* (wood). Have students fill in the chart.

Answers

wood	glass	paper	plastic	metal
5. box	1. bottles	2. book	4. supermarket bags	3. spoon
10. ruler	7. glass	8. newspaper	9. records	6. scissors

7. **Activity 2** Have students use the information in the chart to answer the questions.

Answers   2. It's made of metal.
3. It's made of paper.
4. They're made of metal.
5. They're made of plastic.
6. It's made of wood.
7. They're made of plastic.

Ending the lesson

8. Game: "What's it made of?" Divide the class into two or more teams. Give each team a set time to write down the names of as many objects as they can think of made of each material (glass, paper, metal, plastic, wood) in turn.

9. (Extra) Game: "Guess the Object." Tell students: *I'm thinking about something in the room. It's made of plastic.* Have students take turns asking: *Is it [your pen]?* The first student to guess correctly gets the next turn.

Lesson Two

Language focus
Review: Asking for and giving reasons: *Why? Because ...*

New words
move   surprise (noun)   nice   different   other

Review/Warm-up

1. Review *made of*: Ask: *What's ... made of?* about objects in the room.
- Pair work: Have students ask and answer similar questions.

Story presentation (STUDENT BOOK p.6, CS6)

2. *Magixo the Robot.* The story so far: Uncle John and the children have traveled to Mars in the future to look for the magic book, the Book of Adabra.
- Before listening: Ask questions about the story so far: *Where are Uncle John and the children now?* (Mars) *How did they go to Mars?* (in the Time Machine) *What's the date on the calendar in the Time Machine?* (2060).
- Write focus questions on the board:
  a. What's the name of the robot magician? (Magixo)
  b. What is Magixo made of? (metal and glass)
  c. Who needs Uncle John's help? (Magixo)
  d. What does Magixo show them? (the Book of Adabra)
- Books open. Play CS6. Have students listen and read.
- Play CS6 again. Have students find the answers to the focus questions.
- After listening: Have individuals give answers to the focus questions.
- Ask students to guess the meaning of *What a nice surprise!* from the context. Say: *I'm a magician. I am going to take something out of [Maria's] bag.* Pretend to produce something, and look at it with surprise and delight. Say: *What a nice surprise! It's an ice cream cone!* Then have students role play similar "magic tricks."

- Ask further questions about the story: *Did Kate like the city?* (no) *Why not?* (it was cold) *What was Magixo's rabbit made of?* (metal) *What did Magixo need?* (an Earth magician) *Who is an Earth Magician?* (Uncle John) *Is Magixo a nice robot?* (no)

Story practice

3. Dialogue: Give students copies of the dialogue from the story. Ask them, working in groups, to find out who is speaking by referring to the story. Then have them write down the names of the speakers on the script.

_____: Brr! It's very cold here. I don't like this city.
_____: Don't worry! Follow me!
_____: What's this? It's not moving. It's made of metal and glass … It's a statue.
_____: No. It's a machine … a robot!
_____: Good evening, Earth People. My name is Magixo.
_____: Magixo? Are you a magician?
_____: Yes, I AM a magician … Watch!
_____: Look! It's a robot rabbit!
_____: Well, 4, 5, 6 … SHAZAM!
_____: Aah! What a nice surprise … an Earth magician. I need an Earth magician.
_____: Oh. Why do you need an Earth magician?
_____: Because I need your help. Follow me. I want to show you something.
_____: Uncle John! Look!
_____: Aah! Yes, it is … It's the Book of Adabra.

- Check students' answers. Discuss the feelings of the people in the story. Then have students in groups of five read and practice the story dialogue, taking the parts of Ken, Caroline, Kate, Uncle John, and Magixo.
- Have one or two groups act out the dialogue, including appropriate actions.

4. Summary completion: Write on the board: *Uncle John and the children were at a … on Mars. It was very … They met a … He was made of … and … He … Uncle John's help.*
Ask students to tell you the missing words.

Presentation (STUDENT BOOK p.7)

5. Which one is different? Books closed. Pre-teach *different*. Demonstrate with objects in the classroom: *These pencils are red. This one is different. It is blue.* Ask questions about other items: *Which [bag] is different? Show me.* Pre-teach *other, others.* Say: *Three pencils are red and the other is blue./This ruler is made of plastic and the others are made of wood,* etc.

- Practice *Why?* and *Because.* Ask: *Why did Uncle John build a Time Machine?* (Because he wanted to go to Mars.) *Why did he want to go to Mars?* (Because he wanted to find the Book of Adabra.) *Why did Magixo need an Earth magician?* (Because he needed some help.)
- Books open. Look at the pictures. Ask: *What are these?* for each group of objects in the pictures. Read the sample dialogue out loud.

6. Ask: *Which … is different?* about the other groups of objects (kites, dogs, houses, bicycles). Help students with the answers.

Answers B Number 3. Because it's red and green and the other ones are blue and green. Because it has a long tail and the others don't. C Number 2. Because it's small and the other ones are big. Because it has long ears and the others have short ears. D number 3. Because it's made of wood and the other ones are made of stone. Because it has a red door and the others have blue doors. E Number 1. Because it's pink and the other ones are purple. Because it has a basket and the others don't.

Practice (STUDENT BOOK p.7)

7. Pair work: Have students practice the questions and answers in pairs.

Reading and writing (WORKBOOK p.6)

8. Activity ③ Have students read the story in their Student Book again and circle the correct answer.

Answers 1. right 2. wrong 3. right 4. wrong
5. right

9. Activity ④ Have students read the descriptions and write the names of the mystery objects. This activity can be done as pair work.

Answers 1. a pen 2. chocolate 3. money
4. a milk shake 5. postcards

Ending the lesson

10. Game: "Which one is different?" In groups, have students make collections of objects, e.g., pens, coins, combs, and challenge students from other groups to tell them which object is different, and why. Ask them to write sentences about selected groups of objects.

Be prepared!

Bring materials for drawing.

UNIT 2

Lesson Three

Language focus
Review: Present simple.

New words
astronaut fuel float gravity helmet powder send out (verb) space shuttle space suit tank (=container) difficult work (verb)

Review/Warm-up

1. Game: "Which one is different?" Use objects in the classroom.

2. Review known space vocabulary: *Earth, Moon, satellite, space, rocket.*

Reading (STUDENT BOOK p.8)

3. *Inside a space shuttle.* Ask questions about jobs: *What do police officers do? What do they wear?* Pre-teach *work.* Say: *Police officers work in a police station. Where do teachers/doctors/TV cameramen work?* Pre-teach *gravity* and *float* by translation. Pre-teach *difficult* by miming trying to open the top of a jar of jelly which refuses to come off easily.
- Books open: Pre-teach *fuel tank, helmet, space suit* by referring to the pictures on p.8
- Write focus questions on the board:
  a. What is a space shuttle? (an airplane with two rockets and a fuel tank)
  b. Where can a space shuttle go? (up into space and down again)
  c. Who wears space suits and helmets? (astronauts)
  d. Where do they wear space suits and helmets? (outside the space shuttle)

4. Have students read alone or in pairs. Go around the class, helping students with difficult words. (If students have forgotten what satellites are, show them the ones on p.8 of *American Chatterbox* Student Book 3.)
- After reading. Say: *Point to the rockets. Point to the fuel tank*

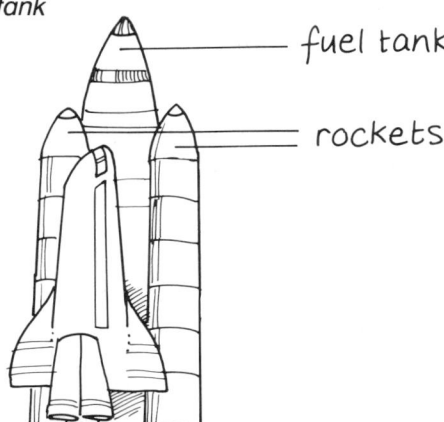

- Have students answer the focus questions on the board.
- Ask students to guess the meanings of *space shuttle, astronaut, send out* from the context.
- Have students write answers to the questions in the book.

Answers
1. It is an airplane with two rockets and a fuel tank.
2. They send out satellites and look at life in space.
3. Because in space there isn't any gravity.
4. No, they don't.
5. It is usually made of powder.

5. Ask further questions about the texts: *Where do astronauts work?* (in the space shuttle) *What do they wear outside the space shuttle?* (space suits and helmets) *What do they do inside the space shuttle?* (They work and eat and sleep.) *What do they eat?* (food made of powder) *What do they add to the food?* (water)

Reading and writing (WORKBOOK pp.7–8)

6. WB p.7 Activity ⑤ Have students look at the pictures and complete the sentences, saying what the different people need.

Answers
2. He needs a calculator.
3. She needs a bag.
4. He needs an umbrella.
5. He needs some glue.

- Pair work: Have students ask and answer questions about the pictures: *What does he need? He needs ...,* etc.

7. **Activity** ⑥ Have students write the characters' words in the speech bubbles. Explain that only the words actually spoken are needed, and that there should be no quotation marks.

Answers

8. **WB p.8 Activity ⑦** Have students read and match the questions and answers

Answers 1. e 2. d 3. a 4. f 5. b 6. c

9. **Activity ⑧** Have students find ten space shuttle words (from SB p.8) in the word search square. This activity may be done as a competition, with the first student to find all ten words being the winner.

Answers

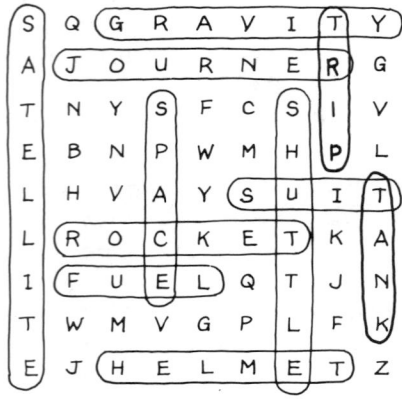

Ending the lesson

10. (Extra) Drawing: Get students to draw and label a picture of a space shuttle in space, using the information on SB p.8.

11. (Extra) Space Project: Ask students to collect more information about space, and help them make scrapbooks or wall displays with pictures drawn or cut out and labeled.

UNIT 3

Lesson One

Language focus
Making rules: *must/must not + before/after/when ...*

New words
bedtime   cabinet   exercises (physical)   *meal   packet
put back   rules*

Review/Warm-up

1. Play the "Please and Thank You" game (see *American Chatterbox* 1, Unit 6, Lesson 2). Include the verb *touch*: *Please touch your ear*, and the expression *made of*: *Please touch something made of glass*, etc.

2. Review meals: *breakfast, lunch, dinner*, and times. Say: *Lunch is a meal. What are the other meals?* Ask: *What time do you have breakfast? When do you have lunch? Do you have dinner at [eight] o'clock?*, etc.

Presentation (STUDENT BOOK p.9)

3. *Uncle John's rules.* Pre-teach new words. Demonstrate *put back* with objects in the classroom. Take something out of its usual storage place and then put it back. Say: *I'm putting [the books] back [in the bookcase]. Please put your [pencil] back [in your bag], [Maria].* Pre-teach *bedtime.* Ask: *What time do you go to bed, [George]?* Say: *[George's] bedtime is ... When's your bedtime?* Demonstrate *exercises.* Say: *I'm doing some exercises.*
• Review *before* and *after.* Ask: *Do you have lunch after you have breakfast? Do you do exercises before breakfast? What do you do before bedtime?*, etc.

4. Books open: Ask questions about the pictures: A. *What's Caroline going to touch?* (the computer buttons) B. *What are they doing? Are they doing exercises?* (yes) C. *What are they putting on?* (space suits and helmets) D. *Are they sleeping?* (no) *Is it bedtime?* (yes) E. *Where are the packets of food?* (in the cabinet) *Who's putting them back in the cabinet?* (Kate and Caroline) F. *What's Uncle John checking?* (the computer) *Is he checking the calendar?* (no) *Who's checking the calendar?* (Kate)

5. Read and match: Read the first rule out loud. Have students find the picture which matches the rule. Then have them read silently and work in pairs to match the rules and pictures.
• Have students read aloud and point.

Answers   1. E   2. F   3. B   4. C   5. A   6. D

UNIT 3

- Ask students to guess the meaning of *rules* from the context. Explain that *you must/you must not* is a way of expressing rules.

Practice (STUDENT BOOK p.9)

6. Ask questions about Uncle John's rules: *When must they put the food packets back in the cabinet? (after breakfast, lunch, and dinner/after meals). When must they check the computers? (before breakfast). When must they not talk or laugh? (after bedtime). When must they not touch the computer buttons? (when Uncle John is outside the Time Machine). When must they put on a space suit? (before they go out into space). When must they do some exercises (after lunch).*

7. Books closed: Write some scrambled sentences on the board:
1. After You exercises lunch. do must some
2. or bedtime. talk laugh You not after must
3. outside not Machine. You buttons Time touch John must when the Uncle computer is
Have students work in groups to sort out the sentences and then write them in the correct order.

Reading and writing (WORKBOOK p.9)

8. Activity ① Have students write *must* or *must not*.

Answers 1. must 2. must 3. must not 4. must not
5. must not 6. must

9. Activity ② Have students look at the pictures and then complete the sentences.

Answers
1. You must not eat ice cream here.
2. You must not go/walk on the grass.
3. You must put your umbrella here.
4. You must not bring your dog here.
5. You must not play baseball here.
6. You must wash your hands before you eat.

Ending the lesson

10. (Extra) Mime: Have students pretend that they are the people in the Time Machine. Have them mime actions, e.g., putting the food packets away. Other students must guess what time of day it is.

11. In groups, have students write rules for the classroom, e.g., *You must clean the board before you go out of the classroom.* Help students with words and expressions they do not know. Discuss the rules with the whole class. Have students choose the best rules and make a list for the classroom wall.

Lesson Two

Language focus
Review: Expressing ability: *can/can't.*

New words
be   dark (noun)   forgot (past tense)   get (= obtain)
mine (possessive)   planet   speak

Review/Warm-up

1. Review *must* and *must not:* Write a list of verbs on the board: *sit, stand, run, eat, sleep.* Have students in pairs or groups, make up rules to go with these: *You must not sit on the table,* etc.

Story presentation (STUDENT BOOK p.10, CS7)

2. *The backward spell.* The story so far: Uncle John and the children have traveled to Mars in the Time Machine to find the Book of Adabra. They have met a robot magician, Magixo, who wants Uncle John's help. Magixo shows them the Book of Adabra.

- Before listening: Ask questions about the story so far: *Where are Uncle John and the children? (on Mars). What is Magixo? (a robot). What does he want? (Uncle John's help). What does he show them? (the Book of Adabra).*
- Pre-teach *forgot.* Say: *I don't have my umbrella today. It's at home. I forgot it.* Write *forget — forgot* on the board. Pre-teach *mine. This is my bag. It's mine.* Point to student's [bag]. Ask: *Is that my [bag], [Maria]?* Help student to answer: *No, it's mine.* Practice with other objects in the classroom. Pre-teach *planet:* translate, and then ask: *Is Mars a planet? Is Earth a planet?*
- Write focus questions on the board:
  a. Can Magixo open the box?   (No, he can't.)
  b. Can Earth people talk backward?   (Yes, they can.)
  c. Why does Magixo want the Book of Adabra? (Because it has strong magic in it.)
  d. Does Uncle John want to help Magixo?   (No, he doesn't.)
  e. Can they get out of the cage?   (No, they can't.)
  f. What did Uncle John forget?   (his magic wand)

- Books open. Play CS7. Have students listen and read.
- Play CS7 again. Have students listen and answer the questions.

Story practice

3. Ask further questions about the story: *Who wanted to be King of the Nine Planets? (Magixo) Why was Magixo angry? (Because Uncle John didn't want to help him.) Who brought the magic wand? (Barker) What did Ken say to Barker? ("Smart dog!") When did the box open? (When Uncle John said the spell backward.)*

4. Give students copies of the story script. Have students find out and write down the names of the speakers.

_____ : Yes, it is the Book of Adabra ... and it's MINE! But I can't open the box. Only an Earth magician can open the box.
_____ : Why?
_____ : Because Earth people can talk backward and robots can't. You must say a spell backward. Then the box can open.
_____ : Why do you want the book?
_____ : There is strong magic in the Book of Adabra. I must have it! Then I can be the King of the Nine Planets.
_____ : Oh no, you can't! I'm not going to help you.
_____ : Oh yes, you are!
_____ : Help! We can't get out!
_____ : Quick, Uncle John. Use your magic wand!
_____ : Oh no! It's in the Time Machine. I forgot it!
_____ : Earth magicians are not very smart. You can't escape now. You must stay here. See you later, Earth magician!
_____ : Look! Here's Barker! Smart dog!
_____ : Good dog, Barker, good dog! Now ... 1,2,3 ... SHAZAM!
_____ : We're free!
_____ : Come on. We must get the Book quickly before Magixo comes back.
_____ : Now, the Book of Adabra ... 3,2,1 ... MAZAHS!
_____ : Look! The box is opening!

- Check answers. Have students read and practice the story dialogue.
- Have one or two groups act out the dialogue, including appropriate actions.

5. Write the following excerpt from Kate's diary on the board: *Magixo wanted Uncle John to ... him. Magixo wanted the Book of Adabra ... there was strong ... in it. He wanted to be King of the Nine ... Uncle John did ... want to help Magixo. So Magixo put us in a cage. But ... helped us ... Magixo can't use the Book of Adabra because robots can't ... ...*

Presentation (STUDENT BOOK p.11, CS8)

6. *Magixo, the Robot.* Pre-teach *dark.* Ask: *Can you see at night? Why not?* Say: *You can't see at night because it is dark. You can't see in the dark.* Pre-teach *speak.* Say: *You can speak [students' own language]. You can speak English.* Ask: *Can you speak ...? (Yes, I can./No, I can't.)*
- Books open. Have students work in pairs, matching pictures and sentences.

Answers 1. H 2. C 3. A 4. G 5. E 6. B 7. D 8. F

7. Play CS8. Have students listen and point.

Tapescript

Voice 1: Listen and point.
Voice 2: Magixo is talking. He is saying "Good morning" in three different languages. First he's saying "Good morning" in English, then he's saying "Good morning" in Spanish, then he's saying "Good morning" in Greek.
Magixo wants to read one of Uncle John's spells. But he's getting angry because he can't read the words. Today is Magixo's birthday. He wants to sing "Happy birthday," but he can't sing! He's making a terrible noise – his rabbit doesn't like it!
Magixo is a clever robot magician. He can do twenty magic tricks. Look at this trick with the rabbit.
Magixo wants to fly through space. But his robot body is made of metal. It's too heavy ... he's going to crash ... No. Magixo can't fly.
Magixo is at the swimming pool on Mars. He's wearing a swimming suit, but he can't swim ... He's going under the water ... somebody help him... quickly!

Practice (STUDENT BOOK p.11)

8. Play CS8 again. This time, stop the tape after each description, and get students to tell you what Magixo can and cannot do.

UNIT 3

- Draw this chart on the board. Have students copy and fill in the chart.

	Magixo		You	
	can	can't	can	can't
speak English				
speak Spanish				
speak Greek				
swim				
fly				
do magic				
sing				
read				
see in the dark				
move forward and backward				

Reading and writing (WORKBOOK p.10)

9. **Activity ③** Have students read the story in the Student Book again, and circle the correct answer.

Answers 1. right 2. right 3. wrong 4. wrong 5. wrong

10. **Activity ④** Have students complete the speeches in the bubbles, using *must*. Do the answers orally before students write the words in the bubbles.

Answers
1. You must stop at this corner!
2. Shhh! We must be quiet. This is a hospital!
3. You must put on your helmet before you leave.
4. You must take two pills before you go to bed.

Ending the lesson

11. Pair work: Have students use the completed *can/can't* chart as the basis of a class survey to find out how many people can do different things. Ask students to suggest other items for the list, e.g., *play tennis/ride a bicycle*.

Lesson Three

Language focus
Review: Present simple.
Review: Expressing ability: *can/can't*

New words
body   get (= become)   program   stories   understand
useful   wheel

Review/Warm-up

1. Ask students to list ways in which they are different from Magixo. Get students to make sentences, e.g., *Magixo can see in the dark, but we can't see in the dark. We can read, but Magixo can't read.* Write the sentences on the board.

Reading (STUDENT BOOK p.12)

2. *Robots.* Books open. Before reading, ask students to point to the robots in the pictures. Say: *Point to the robots. These robots are from Star Wars.* (students point) *This robot is playing the piano. This robot is working in a factory. This robot is drawing pictures.* Ask: *Which robots have legs?* Pre-teach *wheel* by showing examples in the pictures. Pre-teach *computer program* by translation. Pre-teach *body.* Say: *I am drawing a body. See, here is the head, and here are the arms and legs.* Then say: *Magixo cannot swim because his body is made of metal.*

- Have students read the whole story silently. Then read the story out loud, pausing to ask students to point to the relevant details in the pictures.
- Ask students to try to guess the meanings of *useful* and *understand* from the context.

3. After reading: Pair work: Have students find the answers to the questions.

Answers
1. R2D2 and C3P0
2. No, they don't. They usually move around on wheels.
3. No, they do not have a brain and they cannot think.
4. They do dangerous and dirty jobs.
5. No, they never get tired.

Reading and writing (WORKBOOK pp.11–12)

4. WB p.11 **Activity ⑤** Have students answer the questions using the words in the boxes. Do the questions and answers orally before students write.

Answers 2. Because they're in a cage.
3. Because they're too heavy.
4. Because they don't have any legs.
5. Because Barker is barking loudly.

5. Activity ⑥ Have students complete the sentences, writing what the people in the picture said. Remind students to use quotation marks.

Answers 2. Uncle John said, "I forgot my key."
3. Caroline said, "I forgot my umbrella."
4. Kate said, "I forgot my bathing suit."

6. WB p.12 Activity ⑦ Robot quiz. Have students write the answers to the questions.

Answers 1. Marbles are made of glass.
2. Because they can do dangerous and dirty jobs.
3. English.
4. They're made of plastic.
5. You must/have to brush your teeth/wash your face.
6. French.

Ending the lesson

7. Team game: "Robot quiz." Divide the class into two teams. Each team must write down six questions about robots (they can include questions about Magixo in the story), using the pattern *Can [robots/Magixo/...] + action?* Check the questions for correctness and fairness. Then each team chooses a member of the opposite side to answer the question. A correct answer scores a point.

UNIT 4

Lesson One

Language focus
Comparatives: adjective + *er* ... *small – smaller*.

New words
bigger longer nearer older smaller taller thinner younger line

Review/Warm-up

1. Review adjectives: Write on the board, in random order, *long, big, small, young, old, short, fat, thin, happy, sad.* Ask students to find pairs of opposites among them.

Presentation (STUDENT BOOK p.13)

2. Tall ... taller ... Books open: Say: *Point to the two girls with violins. Point to the two dogs. Point to the two giraffes. Point to the two houses. Point to the two bats. Point to the two women.* Students point. Say: *Look at picture A.* Read out loud: *This dog is old. But this dog is older.* Have students point to the two dogs in turn. Write *old – older* on the board. Say: *Look at picture D. Are the girls young or old? (They're young.)* Encourage students to say: *This girl is young. But this girl is younger* — as they point to the appropriate pictures. Write *young – younger* on the board. Continue in the same way with the other pictures. A. *old – older* B. *small – smaller* C. *tall – taller* D. *young – younger* E. *big – bigger* F. *thin – thinner*.

- Draw students' attention to the spelling of *bigger* and *thinner*.

3. Pair work: Have students talk about the pictures in paris.

Practice (STUDENT BOOK p.13)

4. Ask and answer: Practice the first question: *Which line is longer? A or B?* Students answer: *B is longer.*

- Ask students about the other pictures. The picture of a "woman" is an optical illusion which in fact shows an old woman and a young woman in profile. The answer to the question: *Which penguin is nearer to you?* is: *Penguin B.* The answer to the question: *Which mouse is bigger?* is: *They're the same.*
- Pair work: Have students ask and answer questions about the pictures.

UNIT 4

5. Transfer: Get students to ask each other about things and people in the classroom: *Who is taller? [George] or [Maria]? Which desk is nearer to you?*, etc.

Reading and writing (WORKBOOK p.13)

6. Activity ① Have students look at the pictures and then answer the questions, A or B.

Answers   1. B 2. A 3. A 4. B 5. A 6. B 7. B 8. A

- As further practice, have students ask and answer questions about the pictures.

7. Activity ② Transfer: Have students answer questions about each other. Check the answers of individual students by asking the same questions orally.

Ending the lesson

8. Team game: "General knowledge quiz." Divide the class into two teams. Ask each team to make up ten general knowledge questions, which could be questions about the area in which they live: *Which town is bigger? … or …?* Write a list of adjectives on the board to help them: *nearer, longer, bigger, smaller, older, shorter, taller*. Teams take turns asking questions, and a correct answer scores a point.

Lesson Two

Language focus
Review: Comparatives: *more* + adjective.

New words
colorful   mean   shout   problem   than   told (past tense)

Review/Warm-up

1. Ask questions using comparatives about people and things in the classroom: *Who's taller? [George] or [Maria]? Whose bag is bigger? [George's] or [Maria's]? Whose desk is nearer to the window?*
- Write a list of adjectives from Lesson One on the board. Ask students to come to the board and write the comparative form next to each adjective.

Story presentation (STUDENT BOOK p.14, CS9)

2. *The Book of Adabra!* The story so far: Uncle John and the children have escaped from the magic cage made by the robot magician, Magixo. Uncle John has used a spell to get the Book of Adabra. Magixo wants the book because it contains strong spells.

- Before listening: Ask questions about the story so far: *Where are Uncle John and the children? (On Mars) Who wants the Book of Adabra? (Magixo).*
- Pre-teach new word *mean*. Ask: *Is Magixo a nice robot? (no).* Say: *No, he's a mean robot.*
- Ask students questions to predict what will happen next: *Is Uncle John going to help Magixo? (no) Is Magixo going to be happy? (no) Are Uncle John and the children going to stay on Mars? (no).*
- Write focus questions on the board:
  a. Does Magixo catch them again?   (no)
  b. Do they go forward or backward in time? (backward)
  c. What kind of spells are in the Book of Adabra? (very old spells)
  d. Which is older? The Book of Adabra or the Parthenon?   (The Book of Adabra)
  e. What's missing?   (some pages from the book)
- Books open: Play CS9. Have students listen and read.
- Play CS9 again. Have students answer the focus questions.
- Ask students to try to guess the meanings of *shout* and *told* from the context.
- Ask about the rest of the story: *How did Magixo feel? (very angry) Why did Uncle John say a spell? (Because he wanted the Time Machine to come.) Who told Uncle John about the book? (his father) Were the missing pages important? (yes)*

Story practice

3. Dialogue: Give students copies of the story script. Have students find out and write down the names of the speakers.

_____: Aah! We have the Book of Adabra. Now I can read it.

_____: No, not now! Let's go. Come on, Uncle John! Quickly!

_____: We're too late! Magixo is coming. I can see him. What are we going to do?

_____: Quick, Uncle John! Say a spell. Bring the Time Machine here.

_____: 11, 12, 13 … SHAZAM!

_____: Hurray! The Time Machine's here!

_____: Come on, everybody. Let's go!

_____: Come back, Earth magician! That book is mine. You can't take it!

_____: Oh yes, we can! Goodbye, Magixo!

_____: I didn't like Magixo. He was mean!

_____: Look! We're going backward now. It's 1999.

_____: Tell us about the Book of Adabra.

_____: It's a very famous book. My father was a magician and he told me about the book. The spells are very old and the magic is very strong.

_____: How old is the book?

_____: Very, very old. It's older than the Parthenon in Greece, and that's 2,400 years old.

_____: Uncle John. Some pages are missing. Look!

_____: Oh no!

_____: Are the missing pages important, Uncle John?

_____: Every page in the Book of Adabra is important.

_____: But where are the missing pages? Who has them?

- Check students' answers. Then have students practice the story dialogue in groups.
- Have one or two groups act out the dialogue. Draw students' attention to expressions in the story such as *Uncle John said quickly* and *he (Magixo) shouted*, which students should try to do as they act out the story.

4. Write a page from Kate's diary on the board. Have students fill in the blanks. *We got the ... Magixo was very ... and he tried to ... us. Uncle John said a ... and the ... came. Then we went ... to 1999. Uncle John ... us about the Book of Adabra. it is very, very ... But some ... were missing. They are very ... We must ... them.*

Presentation (STUDENT BOOK p.15)

5. *Careful ... more careful ...* Pre-teach *problem* by writing an addition problem on the blackboard. Pre-teach *colorful* by pointing to an appropriate object or picture. Pre-teach *than*. Ask: *Who is taller? [George] or you?* Say: *[George] is taller than you.* Write the sentence on the board, underlining the word *than*. Ask: *Is an elephant bigger than a tiger? Is Magixo smaller than Ken?*, etc.

6. Books open: Say: *Which word is wrong? Point to it.* Have students point to the word crossed out in the picture. Explain that long words cannot add *er* because they would be difficult to say. Instead they have *more* in front of them.

Practice (STUDENT BOOK p.15)

7. Ask and answer: Pair work. Do the first question with the whole class. Ask: *Which trick is more dangerous? Show me.* Students point. Drill the answer: *This trick is more dangerous.*

- Have students continue to ask and answer in pairs.

Reading and writing (WORKBOOK p.14)

8. Activity ③ Reference: Have students carefully read the story in their Student Book again and then answer the questions.

Answers
1. The Book of Adabra
2. Magixo
3. Magixo
4. Uncle John's father
6. the missing pages

9. Activity ④ Have students read and match the verbs with their past tense forms by drawing lines.

Answers   see/saw, make/made, fall/fell, catch/caught, laugh/laughed, cry/cried, ask/asked, write/wrote, do/did, come/came, win/won, dream/dreamed, drop/dropped, send/sent, weigh/weighed, buy/bought, meet/met, give/gave, take/took, find/found

Ending the lesson

10. Review comparatives: Write on the board a selection of adjectives: *small, thin, important, tall, dangerous, colorful, young, big.* Have students come to the board and write either *er* or *more* to change the adjectives into comparatives.

11. (Extra) Have students compare the stamps in the picture on SB p.4: *Which is bigger/smaller/more colorful/more interesting? The [Australian] stamp or the [Russian] stamp? (The [Australian] stamp is ...)*

Lesson Three

Language focus
Review: Describing situations and scenes: *There are ...*

New words
Mercury   Venus   Jupiter   Saturn   Uranus   Neptune Pluto   air   live (= exist)   *solar system   perhaps*

Review/Warm-up

1. Review: *there is ... /there are ...* with objects in the classroom. Ask: *How many [chairs] are there in the classroom? (There are ...)* have students ask and answer in pairs.

UNIT 4

2. Review space vocabulary: *planet, Earth, Mars, the Sun,* Ask: *Is the Earth a planet? Is Mars a planet? Is the Sun a planet?*

Reading (STUDENT BOOK p.16, CS10)

3. *The Planets.* Before reading: Pre-teach the names of the planets, *solar system, air,* and the verb *live* by translation. Explain that *perhaps* means *maybe.*
- Books open. Have students read alone or in pairs. Go around helping the weaker students.

4. After reading: Go through the reading passage again, asking questions: *How many planets are there? (nine) Which planet is next to the Sun? (Mercury) How far is the Earth from the Sun? (93 million miles) Which is bigger? Saturn or the Earth? (Saturn) Does Saturn have air and water? (no) Are there animals on Venus? (no)*

5. Listen and point: Play CS10. Have students listen and point to the right planet.

Tapescript

Answers

Voice 1: Listen and point to the right planet.
Voice 2: This planet is between Jupiter and Uranus. It has beautiful circles around it.
(Saturn)
This planet is bigger and heavier than all the other planets in the solar system.
(Jupiter)
This planet is nearer to the Sun than Venus. It is only 58 million kilometers from the Sun. It is a small planet – smaller than the Earth.
(Mercury)
This planet is between Venus and Mars. It is 150 million kilometers from the Sun. Animals and people can live here because there is air and water on this planet.
(Earth)

Reading and writing (WORKBOOK pp.15–16)

6. WB p.15 **Activity** (5) Have students choose past tense verbs to complete the sentences in the story. The class should do the first sentence together.

Answers
1. traveled, arrived
2. were, wanted
3. said, turned, wanted
4. were, put, sent

- Ask and answer questions about the story: *When did Magixo come from Mars?,* etc.

7. **Activity** (6) Spelling: Have students complete the words.

Answers   1. pick   2. rocket   3. socks   4. ticket   5. clock

8. WB p.16 **Activity** (7) Have students answer the questions in the quiz, reading SB p.16 to find the answers.

Answers
1. nine.
2. the solar system.
3. the Earth.
4. 58 million kilometers.
5. Four: Venus, Mars, Mercury, and Pluto.
6. Four: Jupiter, Saturn, Neptune, and Uranus.

9. **Activity** (8) Have students find the names of the Sun and the planets in the planet.

Answers

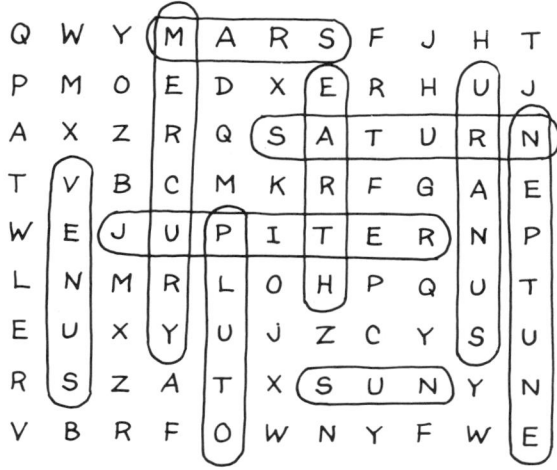

Ending the lesson

10. (Extra) Drawing and writing: Have students draw and label a picture of the solar system, including a short description of each planet.

Be prepared!

Bring a selection of small, almost identical objects, e.g., small stones, one for each student.

UNIT 5

Lesson One

Language focus
Talking about jobs.
Review: Present simple.

New words
center doctor driver experiment farm farmer fire engine fire fighter fire station garage homemaker look after mechanic office put out (= extinguish) repair (verb) secretary sell (verb) sheep salesperson type (verb)

Review/Warm-up

1. Review comparatives: Have students sit in groups. Give each student an object, e.g., a small stone or a button. Have students examine and describe their own object: *My [stone] is bigger/heavier/darker/more colorful than your [stone].* Then, with eyes closed, students mix their objects together. Each student must then find his or her own object again.

Presentation (STUDENT BOOK p.17)

2. *Jobs.* Books open. Pre-teach jobs: *doctor, bus driver, farmer, fire fighter, homemaker, mechanic, salesperson, secretary.* Write the list of jobs on the board and the translation beside them.
- Books open: Say: *Look at the pictures. Show me fire fighters.* Students point. Continue with all the jobs on the list, and include the job that students already know, *scientist.*
- Pre-teach *experiment, farm, fire engine, fire station, garage, office, sheep, type* (verb), by referring to the pictures. Pre-teach *center* by translation.
- Say: *I'm a teacher. I work in a school. I teach you English.*

3. Read and match: Pair work: Have students read and match the sentences with the pictures.

Answers   1. H 2. F 3. A 4. G 5. C 6. B 7. D 8. E

- Ask students to try to guess the meanings of *look after, repair, put out,* and *sell* from the context.

Practice (STUDENT BOOK p.17, CS11)

4. Books open: Listen and point. Play CS11. Have students listen.
- Play CS11 again. Have students listen and point.

Tapescript

Voice 1:   Listen and point.
Voice 2:   He works in a garage. He repairs cars.
She works in a laboratory. She does experiments.
He works on a big farm. He drives a tractor.
She works in an office. She types letters on a computer.
He works in the fire station and on the fire engine. He puts fires out.
He works on a bus. He drives around the center of the city.
She works in a hospital. She helps people.
She works in a clothing store. She sells jeans and shirts.

- Play CS11 again. Have students listen and say the names of the people who do the jobs described.
- Ask further questions about the people and their jobs: *Who works on a big farm? (Stephen) Who repairs cars? (Peter),* etc.

5. Ask and answer: Practice the question and answer in the Student Book with the whole class. *What does your mother do? She's a homemaker. She works in the house. She cleans the rooms and she buys the food.*
- Pair work: Get students to ask and answer questions about the people in the pictures: *What does Jane do?,* etc.
- Transfer: Have students ask and answer questions about their own parents. Help them with the answers where necessary.

Reading and writing (WORKBOOK p.17)

6. **Activity ①** Have students match the pictures and then write sentences.

Answers   2. Judy is going to be a doctor.
3. Lucy is going to be a scientist.
4. Mo is going to be a fire fighter.
5. Susan is going to be a mechanic.
6. Herbie is going to be a farmer.

7. **Activity ②** Have students read the descriptions and then write the answers. Do the first question with the whole class.

Answers   1. He's a salesperson.
2. She's a secretary.
3. She's a scientist.
4. He's a fire fighter.

UNIT 5

Ending the lesson

8. (Extra) Wall display: Ask students to bring pictures (from magazines, etc.) showing different people at work. They can then make a wall display with written captions: *This man is a … He works in a …*, etc.

Lesson Two

Language focus
Talking about jobs.

New words
address   club (Magic Club)   *electricity   good* (friend)
kids (= children)   *lawyer   wonderful*

Review/Warm-up

1. Review jobs: Say: *He's a doctor. Where does he work? (He works in a hospital),* etc. Ask: *What does a fire fighter do? (He puts out fires),* etc. Get students to ask and answer similar questions about the pictures on SB p.17.

Story presentation (STUDENT BOOK p.18, CS12)

2. *The Magic Club.* The story so far: Uncle John and the children have escaped from Mars with the Book of Adabra. But they find that there are some important pages missing from the book.

- Before listening: Ask questions about the story so far: *Did Uncle John and the children escape from Magixo? (yes) Do they have the Book of Adabra? (yes) What is missing? (some pages) Are the missing pages important? (yes).*
- Ask students to predict what will happen next: *What does Uncle John need? (the missing pages) What are they going to try to do? (find the missing pages).*
- Pre-teach new words. Draw an envelope on the board: Say: *This is the stamp. And this is the address.* Pre-teach *electricity* and *lawyer* by translation.
- Write focus questions on the board:
    a. What did Caroline find?   (an envelope with an American stamp, a name, and an address).
    b. Where must they go next?   (to Hollywood).
    c. What does Mr. Lightning do?   (He's a magician and a police officer.)
    d. What kind of magic tricks does Miss Electra do? (tricks with electricity).
- Books open: Listen and read. Play CS12. Have students listen and read.

- Play CS12 again. Have students answer the focus questions.
- Ask students to guess the meanings of *club, good friend, kids,* and *wonderful* from the context.
- Point out the use of the expression: *Hi there, kids!*

Story practice

3. Ask about the rest of the story. *Where was the envelope? (in the Book of Adabra). Whose name was on it? (Lucky Lorenz's). Did Uncle John know Lucky Lorenz? (No, he didn't.) What do they make in Hollywood? (wonderful movies). What are the names of the people at the Magic Club? (Mr. Lightning, Miss Stardust, Miss Electra).*

4. Dialogue: Give students copies of the story script. Ask them to fill in the names of the speakers.

_____: We must find the missing pages.
_____: Look, Uncle John. Here's an envelope. It has an American stamp and a name and address.
_____: Where did you find it?
_____: It was in the Book of Adabra.
_____: Who's Lucky Lorenz?
_____: Lucky Lorenz … I don't know that name. But there's a Magic Club in Hollywood. We can ask the magicians there.
_____: Maybe Lucky Lorenz has the missing pages.
_____: Yes, we must go to Hollywood. We must talk to Lucky Lorenz.
_____: Wow! First we went to Mars … and now we're going to Hollywood. This is great! We're here … in Hollywood! They make wonderful movies here.
_____: Come on! There's the Magic Club, across from the Time Machine. Follow me.
_____: Are all these people magicians?
_____: Yes, but they have other jobs too. Mr. Lightning is a police officer, and Miss Stardust is a doctor. Ah, here's my good friend, Miss Electra.
_____: Hi, John! It's great to see you! Hi there, kids!
_____: Miss Electra, what do you do? Are you a magician all the time, or are you a doctor too … or a lawyer?
_____: I'm a teacher. But on Saturdays I'm a magician. I do magic tricks with electricity!

- Check the answers. Then have students, in groups, take the parts of the characters in the story and

practice reading the story, using appropriate gesture and speed and intonation.
- Have one or two groups act out the story.

5. Draw a postcard from Ken on the board. Have students complete the postcard, with their own names and addresses.

```
We are in Hollywood
now. They ____
wonderful ____ here.
We went to the Magic
____ with Uncle
John. We saw Miss
Electra. She does magic
____ with ____.
See you soon.
                Ken.
```

Song presentation (STUDENT BOOK p.19, CS13)

6. *Tommy is a fire fighter.* Books open: Read out loud the words of the song.
- Play CS13. Have students listen. Ask: *What does Tommy do? What does Sally do? Show me.* Have students mime actions.
- Play CS13 again. Have students join in the song.

Practice (STUDENT BOOK p.19)

7. Play CS13 again. Have students sing and mime the actions.

Reading and writing (WORKBOOK p.18)

8. **Activity ③** Have students read the story in their Student Book again and then complete the questions.

Answers
1. Where did Caroline find the envelope?
2. Whose name and address were on the envelope?
3. Where does Lucky Lorenz live?
4. What do they make in Hollywood?
5. What job does Miss Electra do?

9. **Activity ④** Have students read the addresses on the envelopes and work out what the people's jobs are. Do the first one with the whole class.

Answers
1. Miss Shining Sun is a teacher.
2. Mrs. P.C. Catcher is a police officer.
3. Ms M. Star is an astronaut.
4. Mr. Birdbrain is a scientist.
5. Mr. Wizzo is a doctor.

Ending the lesson

10. Song: *Tommy is a fire fighter.* Sing the song again. Then have students add their own verses to the song, using different names and jobs. Divide class into groups. Each group should contribute a verse.

Lesson Three

Language focus
Review: *Is there a ...?*

New words
builder   cook (noun)   dancer   mail carrier   nurse (noun)
vet (= *veterinarian*)

Review/Warm-up

1. Song: *Tommy is a fire fighter.* Play CS13 again. Have students join in and include their own new verses.

2. Review jobs: Pair work: Write the following scrambled words on the board: RAFREM (farmer), SUB VIDERR (bus driver), CODROT (doctor), WALREY (lawyer), RIFE GIFTHRE (fire fighter), CANICHEM (mechanic), CRESTEARY (secretary), CHERTEA (teacher), CISTSINET (scientist). Have students write down the jobs.

Review/Practice (STUDENT BOOK p.20, CS14)

3. A guessing game: *Who's in your family?* Pre-teach new words: *builder, cook, dancer, nurse, mail carrier, vet.* Write these jobs on the board, and translate them into the students' own language.
- Books open: Say: *Point to the Sanchez family. Point to Maria Sanchez.* Students point. Ask: *What does Maria Sanchez do? (She's a secretary). What does Mr. Sanchez do? (He's a builder),* etc.
- Play CS14. Have students listen and read.

Tapescript

Voice 1:	Listen and read.
Kate:	Choose a family, Ken.
Ken:	OK.
Kate:	Is there a doctor in your family?
Ken:	No, there isn't.
Kate:	Is there a homemaker in your family?
Ken:	No, there isn't.
Kate:	Is your family the Sanchez family?
Ken:	Yes! That's my family. Very good!

UNIT 5

- Have students practice the dialogue in pairs, taking turns playing Kate and Ken.
- Play the game with one of the students. Say: *Choose a family, [George].* Use the same language as Kate and Ken do in the recording.
- Pair work: Have students play the game, taking turns asking and answering.

Reading and writing (WORKBOOK pp.19–20)

4. WB p.19 **Activity (5)** Who lives here? Have students look at the picture and write sentences.

Answers
2. The dancer lives at number 2.
3. The builder lives at number 3.
4. The doctor lives at number 4.
5. The secretary lives at number 5.
6. The farmer lives at number 6.
7. The cook lives at number 7.
8. The artist lives at number 8.

5. Activity (6) Have students read the questions, and refer to the pictures for the answers. This activity may be done as pair work.

Answers   1. the dancer   2. the dancer   3. the cook
4. the mail carrier   5. the secretary and the builder

6. WB p.20 **Activity (7)** Transfer: Have students answer the questions about their own families (*He's a +* job). Go around the class helping students with words they do not know.

7. Activity (8) Have students complete the crossword puzzle with the jobs shown in the pictures.

Answers

Ending the lesson

8. Song: *Tommy is a fire fighter.* Play CS13 again. Have students join in, adding new verses.

9. (Extra) Dialogue: Pair work. Have students practice in pairs, supplying details of their own families.
A: Is there a doctor in your family?
B: Yes, there is./No, there isn't.

Be prepared!

Bring drawing materials.

Testing

Now is an appropriate time to test students on the previous five units.

These suggestions are intended to complement the reading and writing exercises in *American Chatterbox Tests* at the end of this Teacher's Book.

- Spelling: Read aloud the following ten words for students to write and spell.

  1. different   2. surprise   3. understand
  4. colorful   5. thinner   6. address
  7. builder   8. experiment 9. mechanic
  10. wonderful

- Dictation: Read aloud each section of the following dictation twice. Have students listen and write.
  Magixo is a robot./He lives on Mars./He is made of metal./He can see in the dark,/but he can't read.

Read through the whole dictation again for students to listen and check.

- Composition: Ask students to write three or four sentences about the planets in the solar system using prepositions: *near, between, next to.*

- Oral assessment: Students' oral skills and activity are best assessed during normal oral work in class over a period of several lessons. However, if a test is also desirable, take the pictures from one of the story pages, cover the captions and ask questions about what is happening in one or two pictures: *Where are Uncle John and the children? Who said, "..."? What's Uncle John doing?,* etc.

UNIT 6

Lesson One

Language focus
Superlatives: adjective + *est* ... *big – bigger – the biggest*

New words
*best   better   biggest   fattest   happiest   heavier
heaviest   longest   oldest   saddest   shortest   smallest
tallest   thinnest   youngest*

Review/Warm-up

1. Sing *Tommy is a fire fighter* from Unit 5, CS13.

2. Review comparatives: Ask questions about people and objects in the classroom. *Who is taller? [George] or [Maria]? Which is bigger? The red [bag] or the blue one?* Students answer. Then get students to ask questions.

Presentation (STUDENT BOOK p.21)

3. *The Magic Club.* Introduce superlatives: Ask three students to stand at the front of the class. Say: *[George] is tall. [Maria] is taller. [David] is the tallest.* Write *tall – taller – the tallest* on the board. Take three books of different weights: a small hardback book and a very heavy hardback book. Say: *This book is heavy. This book is heavier.* Find a very large, very heavy book and say: *This book is the heaviest.*
- Books open. Look and say. Have students point to the books carried by the boys and say: *heavy – heavier – heaviest.* Then have them point to the three girls and say: *tall – taller – tallest.*
- Say: *Point to Mr. Lightning. Point to Miss Electra.* Students point. Ask: *Is Mr. Lightning a good magician? (yes) Is Miss Electra a better magician? (yes).* Tell students to look at the beginning of the story on the next page to find out who is the best magician. Ask: *Who's the best magician? (Mr. Wizzo)* Write *good – better – best* on the board.
- Ask: *Which girl is the tallest? (This one.)* Students point to the third girl magician. *Which book is the heaviest? Which magician is the best?*

Practice (STUDENT BOOK p.21)

4. Practice the first question and answer with the whole class: *Which magician is the tallest? (Magician B is the tallest.)*
- Pair work: Have students ask and answer the questions in pairs.

Answers
1. G is the shortest; F is the saddest; E is the happiest; C is the thinnest; D is the fattest; A is the oldest; G is the youngest
2. F has the longest hair; G has the shortest hair.
3. D has the biggest hat; F has the smallest hat.

5. Say: *Point to the youngest magician. Point to the magician with the biggest hat,* etc. Have students point.

6. Spelling: Draw students' attention to the spelling of *heavier, heaviest* in which *y* is changed into *i*. Ask them to complete the sequence with *happy, heavy*, and *pretty*. As review, ask them to write out the comparative and superlative forms of *thin, big, fat,* and *sad*.

Reading and writing (WORKBOOK p.21)

7. **Activity 1** Have students find the sets of words in the box and write them down.

Answers   sad/sadder/saddest;   big/bigger/biggest
long/longer/longest;   good/better/best
thin/thinner/thinnest;   fat/fatter/fattest;
short/shorter/shortest;   heavy/heavier/heaviest

8. **Activity 2** Have students look at pictures of the animals and circle the correct answers.

Answers   1. right   2. wrong   3. right   4. right   5. right
6. wrong   7. wrong   8. wrong   9. right

Ending the lesson

9. Transfer: Group work: In groups, have students make up lists of superlatives about the children in the class: *[David] is the tallest. [George] is the youngest. [Maria] has the longest hair,* etc.

10. Drawing and writing: Group work: Have students make drawings for the classroom wall to illustrate superlatives: *big – bigger – biggest; small – smaller – smallest,* etc.

Be prepared!

Bring paper for writing and drawing to the next lesson.

UNIT 6   **29**

Lesson Two

Language focus
Superlative *the most* + adjective.

New words
fantastic   help (noun)   *horse   jaguar   mask   most   piece*

Review/Warm-up

1. Practice superlatives: Ask questions about the magicians in the picture on SB p.21: *Which magician is the saddest? (Magician F is the saddest)*, etc.

Story presentation (STUDENT BOOK p.22, CS15)

2. *The oldest magician.* The story so far: Uncle John and the children are in Hollywood. They want to find the missing pages from the Book of Adabra. They are visiting the Magic Club.
- Before listening: Ask questions about the story so far: *Where are Uncle John and the children? (in Hollywood) Who do they want to find? (Lucky Lorenz) Who's the best magician at the Magic Club? (Wizzo).*
- Pre-teach *piece* using material in the classroom, e.g., paper. Show students three different sized pieces of paper. Ask: *Which piece is the biggest/smallest? (This piece).*
- Write focus questions on the board:
  a. What does Mr. Wizzo give Ken? (a piece of chocolate cake)
  b. Who's the oldest magician in the world? (Mr. Wizzo)
  c. Does Mr. Wizzo know Lucky Lorenz? (yes)
  d. Where is Lucky Lorenz now? (at movie studio ten)
- Books open: Play CS15. Have students listen and read.
- Play CS15 again. Have students listen and then answer the focus questions.

Story practice

3. Ask questions about the story: *What did the children watch? (the Magic Show) Were the children hungry? (yes) Who had the biggest piece of cake? (Ken) What did Uncle John show Mr. Wizzo? (the Book of Adabra) Where is movie studio ten? (opposite the ABC movie theater).* Ask students to guess the meaning of *fantastic* from the context.

4. Dialogue: Give students copies of the story script and ask them to write in the names of the speakers.

_____: You were very good. You were better than Mr. Lightning.
_____: You were the best, Mr. Wizzo!
_____: Your magic tricks were great!
_____: Thank you, Ken. I know a chocolate cake trick too. Are you hungry?
_____: Yes!
_____: Children are always hungry. Watch me ... HEY PRESTO!
_____: Wow! Thank you, Mr. Wizzo.
_____: Hey Ken! You have the biggest piece!
_____: Uh ... yes, I do, but Barker's hungry too. Mr. Wizzo is a fantastic magician!
_____: Yes, he is. And he's the oldest magician in the world too.
_____: How old are you, Mr. Wizzo?
_____: I'm 110!
_____: Now, Mr. Wizzo. Look at this. You're old, but this is older. Look! This is the Book of Adabra.
_____: The Book of Adabra! Where did you find it?
_____: On Mars.
_____: We need your help, Mr. Wizzo. There are some pages missing in the Book of Adabra. But we found this name in the Book. Do you know Lucky Lorenz?
_____: Yes I do. Everybody knows Lucky Lorenz. She's the most famous magician in Hollywood.
_____: Where can we find her?
_____: She's making a movie now. She's at movie studio ten. That's across from the ABC Movie Theater. It's very near here.
_____: OK. Let's go! Thanks, Mr. Wizzo.

- Check students' answers. Then have students act out the dialogue in groups.
- Have one or two groups perform the dialogue for the whole class, using appropriate actions and intonation.

5. Write the following letter from Kate to her mother on the board. Have students fill in the blanks.

```
Dear Mom,
We are in _____ now. We _____ a Magic Show
at the Magic Club. Mr. Wizzo was the _____
magician. He is the _____ magician in
the _____. After the show he _____
us some chocolate _____. Ken had the
_____ piece.
Now we are going to find _____. She is
making a _____ at _____.      Love, Kate.
```

Presentation (STUDENT BOOK p.23)

6. *What do you think?* Books open: Pre-teach new words: *horse, jaguar,* and *mask* by referring to the pictures. Ask students to identify all the other items in the pictures. Say: *Show me the sports. What's this sport? (windsurfing),* etc.

- Read the questions out loud: *Which sport is the most dangerous?,* etc. Explain that with long adjectives the superlative is made with *most*. Write on the board: *big – bigger – biggest/good – better – best/dangerous – more dangerous – most dangerous.*
- Pair work: Have students ask and answer questions about the pictures.

Practice (STUDENT BOOK P.23)

7. Transfer: Have students write sentences, which can be accompanied by drawings: *I think the most dangerous sport in the world is ...,* etc.

Reading and writing (WORKBOOK p.22)

8. Activity ③ Have students read the story in their Student Book again, looking carefully to find the correct form of the sentences.

Answers
1. Mr. Wizzo is the best magician.
2. Ken took/had/ate the biggest piece of Mr. Wizzo's cake.
3. Mr. Wizzo is the oldest magician in the world.
4. The Book of Adabra is older than Mr. Wizzo.
5. Lucky Lorenz is the most famous magician in Hollywood.

9. Activity ④ Have students read the questions and look at the pictures to find the answers.

Answers 1. No 2. Fred 3. Fred's 4. Jill's 5. No 6. Yes 7. No 8. Charlie

- Pair work: Have students ask and answer questions about the pictures.

Ending the lesson

10. (Extra) Have students hold a competition to design a mask. The masks can be judged as the most interesting, the most frightening or the most colorful.

Lesson Three

Language focus
Talking about weights and measures.
Superlatives: *the tallest in the world.*

New words
fastest   inch   land (noun)   *mustache   pound
record   record breaker   run* (verb)   *second* (of time)
ton   weigh (verb)

Classroom English
measure (v)

Review/Warm-up

1. Review superlatives: Ask questions about the story: *Who is the best magician at the Magic Club? (Mr. Wizzo) Who is the most famous magician in Hollywood? (Lucky Lorenz) Who is the oldest magician in the world? (Mr. Wizzo) Who had the biggest piece of choclate cake? (Ken).*

Reading (STUDENT BOOK p.24)

2. *The Guinness Book of Records.* Pre-teach *inch* and review *feet.* Show students a ruler and measure various things in the classroom. Say: *This [pencil] is [7] inches long. Measure your [pencils], please.* Have students measure various things around the classroom. Pre-teach *second.* Say: *There are sixty minutes in one hour. There are sixty seconds in one minute.* Pre-teach *weigh, pound,* and *ton* by translation. Ask: *How much do you weigh? Who is heavier? [George] or [Maria]?* Pre-teach *record* and *record breakers* and *mustache* by translation. Write the new words *inch, feet, second, weigh, pound, ton, record breaker, mustache* on the board.

3. Scanning: Books open. Have students find the words on the board in the reading passage.
- Have students read the passage silently.
- Ask further questions about the reading: *Who is the tallest woman in the world? Who is the heaviest man in the world? Who is the fastest woman in the world? Who has the longest mustache in the world? What is the biggest animal on land?*
- Pair work: Have students write down the answers to the questions in the book.

Answers
1. She is 231 centimeters tall.
2. The fastest woman in the world is Florence Griffith-Joyner.
3. They are 87.18 centimeters tall.
4. It is 318 centimeters long.
5. It weighs 2,250 kilograms.

UNIT 6/7

Reading and writing (WORKBOOK pp.23–24)

4. WB p.23 **Activity** ⑤ Ask students questions about the map: *Where's Studio 2?*, etc. Have students read and answer the questions with full sentences.

Answers
2. Sammy is in Studio 4, across from the park.
3. Sally is Studio 8, next to the bank.
4. Billy is in Studio 2, between the restaurant and the school.
5. Betty is in Studio 5, between the supermarket and the hospital.
6. Bobby is in Studio 9, across from the police station.

5. WB p.24 **Activity** ⑥ Have students answer the questions about themselves and fill in the boxes. Then have them answer the questions, using this information.

6. **Activity** ⑦ Have students answer the questions. Have them answer on their own, then compare their answers with the rest of the class.

Ending the lesson

7. (Extra) Have students write and illustrate their own Book of Records. These could be records about children in the class: *The girl with the longest hair in the class is … Her hair is … inches long*, etc.

8. (Extra) Dialogue: In groups, have students act out interviews with the people from *The Guinness Book of Records*.
   A: Are you the tallest woman in the world?
   B: Yes, I am. My name's Sandy Allen.
   A: How tall are you?
   B: I'm 231 centimeters tall.

UNIT 7

Lesson One

Language focus
Review: Past simple, *going to* future.
Time: *last Friday & next Friday*.

New words
Past tense: *bought   did   met   washed*

Review/Warm-up

1. Review superlatives and weights and measures: Ask: *Who has the heaviest [bag]? Who has the longest hair? Who is the tallest person in the class? How tall is he/she?*

Presentation (STUDENT BOOK p.25)

2. *Wizzo's diary*. Review the days of the week. Ask: *Which day comes after Monday? Which day comes before Friday? Which day comes between Tuesday and Thursday?*, etc.
- Pre-teach new past tense forms and review known forms. Write on the board, in random order: *play, buy, go, wash, send, do, meet, played, bought, went, washed, sent, did, met*. Have students come to the board and draw lines connecting present and past tense forms.
- Review past simple and the *going to* future by asking questions: *Where did you go yesterday? What are you going to do tomorrow? What did you eat for breakfast? What are you going to eat after the lesson?* Write example sentences on the board: *[George] went to [the swimming pool] yesterday. [Maria] is going to [play tennis] tomorrow.*

3. Books open. Say: *This is a diary. Whose diary is it? It's Wizzo's diary. Point to today. Point to yesterday. Point to tomorrow. Point to last Monday. Point to next Friday.*
- Read and match: Pair work: Have students match the pictures with the dates in the diary.

Answers
A. Thursday, March 5.
B. Wednesday, March 11.
C. Wednesday, March 4.
D. Sunday, March 1.
E. Saturday, March 14.
F. Tuesday, March 3.

Practice (STUDENT BOOK p.25, CS16)

4. Ask questions about the diary and pictures: *Did Wizzo meet Uncle John last week? (yes) Did he meet Miss Electra last week? (no) Is he going to meet her this week? (yes) Did he buy a computer last week? (no) What did he buy last week? (a new wand).*
- Listen and point: Play CS16. Have students listen and point.

Tapescript

Voice 1: Listen and point.
Voice 2: What did Wizzo do last Friday?
Voice 3: He sent a postcard to Uncle Paul.
Voice 2: What did Wizzo do last Tuesday?
Voice 3: He met Uncle John at the restaurant.
Voice 2: What did Wizzo do last Thursday?
Voice 3: He washed the car.
Voice 2: What did Wizzo do last Sunday?
Voice 3: He bought a new magic wand.
Voice 2: What is Wizzo going to do next Friday?
Voice 3: He's going to go to the museum.
Voice 2: What is Wizzo going to do next Wednesday?
Voice 3: He's going to wash some clothes.
Voice 2: What is Wizzo going to do next Saturday?
Voice 3: He's going to meet Miss Electra at the café.
Voice 2: What is Wizzo going to do next Monday?
Voice 3: He's going to play tennis.

5. Pair work: Have students take turns asking and answering questions about Wizzo's diary.
- Memory test: Books closed: Ask questions like the ones in the tapescript. Have students try to remember what Wizzo did/is going to do on each day.

Reading and writing (WORKBOOK p.25)

6. Activity ① Have students look at the pictures, and then complete Kate's diary. Ask questions about the pictures first.

Answers   Thursday: We went to school in the morning.
We listened to records in the afternoon.
We watched TV in the evening.

Saturday: We're going to play tennis in the morning.
We're going to meet Caroline in the afternoon.
We're going to make a pizza in the evening.

7. Activity ② Have students answer questions and write about themselves. Ask individual students first: *What did you do in the morning yesterday, [George]?*, etc.

Ending the lesson

8. (Extra) Writing a diary: Group work: Ask each group to choose a character, and write an imaginary diary, using the same days and dates as Wizzo's diary. The character could be someone from *American Chatterbox*, e.g., Uncle John or Magixo, or another favorite character, fictional or real.
- Have students from other groups ask and answer questions about these diaries.

Lesson Two

Language focus
Review: Present continuous.

New words
antelope buffalo cloudy cowboy deer discouraging gun movie director (go) past range roam seldom turn left   You're welcome

Past participle
heard

Review/Warm-up

1. Review past tense verbs. List the present tense forms on the board: *play, go wash, send, do, meet*. Have students come to the board and write the past simple forms.

Story presentation (STUDENT BOOK p.26, CS17)

2. *Cowboy city*. The story so far: The children and Uncle John are in Hollywood. They want to find the missing pages from the Book of Adabra. They are going to meet Lucky Lorenz, the most famous magician in Hollywood.
- Before listening: Ask questions about the story so far: *Who did they meet at the Magic Club? (Mr. Wizzo). Who are they going to meet? (Lucky Lorenz). Where are they going to meet her? (at the movie studio).*
- Pre-teach *go past* and *turn left* by mime.
- Before listening: Books open: Pre-teach *movie director, cowboy,* and *gun* by referring to the pictures.
- Write focus questions on the board:
  a. What is the short cowboy's name?   (Harry Jackson).
  b. Do the cowboys have real guns?   (no).
  c. Where is Lucky Lorenz's room?   (next to studio number 3).
  d. What does Uncle John want to do?   (ask Lucky some questions).

UNIT 7

- Books open: Play CS17. Have students listen and read.
- Play CS17 again. Have students listen and answer the focus questions.
- After listening: Ask students to guess the meaning of *Your welcome* from the context.

Story practice

3. Ask further questions about the story: *What did the short cowboy steal? (the tall cowboy's best horse, money and girl) Were the cowboys really dead? (no) Did the cowboys help Uncle John and the children? (yes) Did Uncle John and the children find Lucky Lorenz? (yes).*

4. Dialogue: Give students copies of the story script. Have students write in the names of the speakers.

_____: Hey, this is exciting. They're making a cowboy movie.
_____: Look at those cameras! I'm going to be cameraman ... or a movie director.
_____: Come on, Ken. Let's watch the cowboys. They have guns!
_____: What are they going to do? Are they ...
_____: Shh! Listen!
_____: You stole my best horse. You stole my money. And you stole my girl. I'm going to kill you, Harry Jackson!
_____: Oh yes?
_____: They're dead! They aren't moving.
_____: Oh no! Uncle John, come here quickly!
_____: It's OK. We're alive.
_____: Don't worry. We're making a movie. These aren't real guns.
_____: Can we help you?
_____: Yes, please. We're looking for Lucky Lorenz.
_____: Lucky Lorenz? OK. Go through that door, and turn left. Go past Mickey Mouse's house, and Lucky's room is next to studio number 3. OK?
_____: OK! And thank you.
_____: You're welcome. Bye now!
_____: Lucky Lorenz? My name is John Jones, and I'm a magician. I want to ask you some questions, please.
_____: OK. Come in.

- Have students practice the dialogue in groups.
- Have one or two groups act out the dialogue.

5. Summary completion: Write an excerpt from Kate's diary on the board. Have students complete it.

Yesterday we went to ...
We saw ...
We watched ...
The cowboys had ...
The cowboys laughed because they weren't ...
We turned ... then we went ...
We found ...

Song presentation (STUDENT BOOK p.27, CS18)

6. *Home on the Range.* Before listening: Books open: Pre-teach new words: *buffalo, deer, antelope, range* by referring to the pictures. Say: *Point to the buffalo. Point to the deer. Point to the antelope.* Teach the meaning of *seldom* by comparing it to the adverbs of frequency (*always, often, sometimes, never*) which students already know. Mime the meaning of *roam*, and *is heard* (past participle). Translate *discouraging*. Explain the meaning of *all day* by saying, *It's [cold] in the morning, in the afternoon and in the evening. It's [cold] all day.*

- Read the song aloud with the class to practice saying the new words.

7. Play CS18. Have students listen.
- Ask students to guess the meaning of *cloudy* from the context. Ask *Is it cloudy today?* (Students already know *cloud*.)
- Play CS18 again. Have students listen and sing.

Practice (STUDENT BOOK p.27)

8. Ask and answer: Ask questions about the song with books open. *Who is singing this song? (a cowboy) Where does he want to live? (on the range) What kind of animals can you find on the range? (buffalo, deer, antelope) What kind of song is this? (a happy song).*

Reading and writing (WORKBOOK p.26)

9. Activity ③ Have students read the story in their Student Book again, then read the sentences. Then have them decide the order in which the sentences should go to tell the story again.

Answers Uncle John took the children to a movie studio in Hollywood.
They saw some movie stars. They were making a cowboy movie.
There was a tall cowboy and a short cowboy in the movie.
The tall cowboy killed the short cowboy with his gun.
The short cowboy stood up again and laughed.
The cowboys' guns were not real.
They found Lucky Lorenz in a room near Studio 3.

10. **Activity ④** Have students read and match the pictures with the words from the cowboy movies.

Answers   1. C   2. A   3. B

Ending the lesson

11. Sing *Home on the Range* again.

Lesson Three

Language focus
Review: Comparatives and superlatives, *made of*, jobs.

New words
child   class   Indian

Review/Warm-up

1. Sing *Home on the Range* again.

Review/Practice (STUDENT BOOK p.28)

2. A game: *Cowboys and Indians*. Before reading. Pre-teach new words: *Indian* (refer students to the pictures on p. 28), *child*, and *class* (students already know *children* and *classroom*). Write these words on the board.
• Scanning: Books open: Ask students to find the words on the board and point to them on SB p.28.

3. Read the instructions out loud. Have students work in pairs, one cowboy and one Indian. Tell students that they can look back in the book to find the answers if they need to. Have students write down the answers.
• As they finish, all the cowboys and all the Indians get together, in different parts of the classroom, to compare their answers. The first group to produce eight correct answers is the winner.

4. Cowboys and Indians, now two teams, challenge each other to answer the other set of questions.

Reading and writing (WORKBOOK pp.27-28)

5. WB p.27 **Activity ⑤** Have students look at the pictures and then write sentences about what is going to happen. Do the answers orally first with the whole class.

Answers
2. Uncle John is going to fall into the swimming pool.
3. The cowboy is going to sit in some paint.
4. A giraffe is going to eat Kate's apple.
5. Spider is going to escape from the prison.
6. Barker is going to eat the cookies.

6. **Activity ⑥** Have students read the statements from the three children and fill in the chart. Check the answers before going on to do the rest of the activity.

Answers

	Number of marbles			
	blue	white	green	total
Kate	16	30	15	61
Judy	14	42	25	81
Jamie	20	40	20	80

• Have students answer the questions, using the figures in the boxes.

Answers   1. Judy and Jamie   2. Jamie   3. Judy   4. Judy

7. WB p.28 **Activity ⑦** Have students use the pictures to help complete the crossword puzzle.

Answers

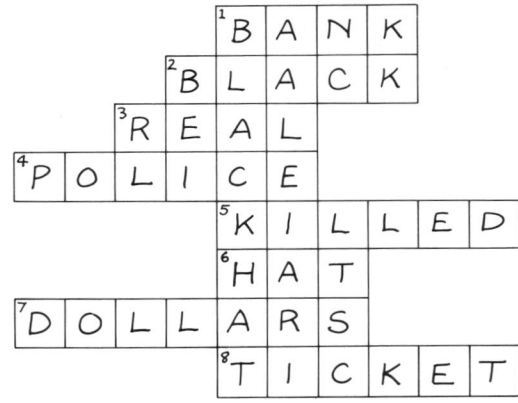

The robber's name is Black Hat.

Ending the lesson

8. (Extra) Team game: Divide the class into two teams. Have students make up questions with superlatives and challenge members of the other team to answer them.

9. Sing the song *Home on the Range* again.

UNIT 8

Lesson One

Language focus
Offering politely: *Would you like ...?*

New words
lemon   potato chips

Review/Warm-up

1. Review past simple and the *going to* future. Ask: *What did you do yesterday? Where did you go yesterday? What are you going to do tomorrow? Where are you going to go tomorow?* Have students answer.

2. Sing *Home on the Range* (CS18) again.

Presentation (STUDENT BOOK p.29)

3. *What would you like to eat?* Pre-teach new word: *lemon* by drawing one on the board. Say: *I don't like lemons, but I like lemon ice cream.* Say: *I'm hungry. I'd like some [chocolate cake]. Would you like some [chocolate cake]?* Ask students to suggest different kinds of food, and make a list on the board. Then ask: *What would you like to eat, [George]?* Have students answer.

4. Books open. Pre-teach *potato chips* by referring students to the pictures. Ask: *What kind of food can you see in the pictures?* Students answer. Have them read the conversation in the book silently. Ask: *What does Uncle John want?* (some green tea) *What does Ken want?* (some black ice cream).
- Have students practice the conversation in groups of three.

Practice (STUDENT BOOK p.29)

5. Books open. Have students identify the foods in the picture. Say: *Point to the frog pizza. Point to the lemon cookies. Point to the potato chips*, etc.
- Ask and answer: Read the dialogue out loud. Have students repeat.
- Pair work: Have students ask and answer, asking questions about all the items in the pictures.

6. Role play: Group work: Ask groups to write a restaurant menu for the Robot Café, in which all the items are made of metal. Groups then act as customers and waiters at their café, using the structure: *Would you like ...? Yes, please./No, thank you.*

Reading and writing (WORKBOOK p.29)

7. **Activity** ① Have students read the menu and write the conversation. Practice the first question and answer orally, and write them on the board.

Answers
2. Would you like some snake steak? No, thank you. I'd like some rope salad.
3. Would you like some fish ice cream?/Yes, please.
4. Would you like some mouse cake or some insect cookies?/I'd like some insect cookies, please.

Ending the lesson

8. Guessing game: "What would you like?" Say: *I'd like to eat something* or *I'd like to drink something*. Have students guess what it is you would like: *Would you like some [ice cream/milk]?*, etc. When a student guesses correctly he/she says: *I'd like to ...*, etc., and the other students guess.

Lesson Two

Language focus
Expressing desire or preference: *I'd like to ...*

New words
bee   build   echo (verb)   *else* (= other)   *for once   furnish   harmony   keep company   love* (noun)   *of course   peace   perfect   snow-white   teach   throughout   turtle dove   unhappy*

Review/Warm-up

1. Review *I'd like ...* with foods. Ask: *Would you like some [frog pizza]?*, etc. Students answer: *Yes, please* or *No, thank you.*

Story presentation (STUDENT BOOK p.30, CS19)

2. *Spider Smith again!* The story so far: Uncle John and the children are in Hollywood. They have found Lucky Lorenz at the movie studio. They want to ask her about the missing pages from the Book of Adabra.
- Before listening: Ask questions about the story so far: *Who is Lucky Lorenz?* (a magician) *Where does she work?* (in a movie studio) *What does Uncle John want to ask her about?* (the missing pages).
- Write focus questions on the board:
  a. Who is Kashoki? (a Japanese magician)
  b. Does he have the missing pages? (no)
  c. Who visited Lucky Lorenz three days ago? (Spider Smith)
  d. Where does Ringo Dingo live? (Australia)

3. Books open. Play CS19. Have students listen and read.
- Play CS19 again. Have students listen and answer the questions on the board.
- Have students guess the meanings of *of course, else,* and *unhappy,* from the context.

Story practice

4. Ask further questions about the story: *What did Uncle John tell Lucky about? (the missing pages) What question did Spider Smith ask? (Who has those pages?) Where did Spider Smith go? (to Australia).*

5. Dialogue: Give students copies of the story script. Have students write in the names of the speakers.

_____	: Wow! I'd like to wear this hat.
_____	: Can we look at your clothes, please?
_____	: Yes, of course. Would you like to put that coat on?
_____	: Yes, please!
_____	: This is very interesting. A long time ago my friend Kashoki had the Book of Adabra. Do you know Kashoki?
_____	: Kashoki, the Japanese magician?
_____	: Yes, that's right. But Kashoki doesn't have the missing pages. I know, because he told me.
_____	: Oh no! Then who has those pages?
_____	: I don't know, but somebody else asked me that question three days ago!
_____	: Who was that?
_____	: His name was Spider Smith.
_____	: Spider Smith! Oh no! We know him.
_____	: But he's in prison.
_____	: Perhaps he escaped from prison. This is bad news. Where is Spider now, Lucky? Do you know?
_____	: Spider went to Australia. He went to Ringo Dingo's house. Spider and Ringo Dingo are working together. They want to find the Book of Adabra and the missing pages.
_____	: This is terrible news! I know Ringo Dingo. He's a bad man.
_____	: Can we go to Australia in the Time Machine?
_____	: Yes. We must find Spider and Ringo Dingo. Goodbye, Lucky, and thank you for your help.
_____	: Goodbye. Be careful! I didn't like Spider Smith.

- Have students, in groups, read and act out the story.
- Have one or two groups perform in front of the class.

6. Sequencing: Pair work: Write the following sentences on the board.
   a. Spider Smith went to Australia.
   b. Uncle John and the children met Lucky Lorenz.
   c. Uncle John told Lucky about the Book of Adabra.
   d. Kashoki had the Book of Adabra.
   e. Spider Smith asked Lucky about the missing pages.
   f. Spider Smith escaped from prison.
- Have students in pairs decide the order in which these events happened.

Answers   1. d   2. f   3. e   4. a   5. b   6. c

Song presentation (STUDENT BOOK p.31, CS20)

7. *I'd like to teach the world to sing.* Books open. Pre-teach new words and expressions: *build, honey bees, keep it company, perfect harmony, peace, love, teach, furnish, echo, for once.* Pre-teach these by translation and write them on the board.
- Tell students to look at SB p.31. Say: *Point to the honey bees. Point to the snow-white turtle doves.* Students point.
- Scanning: Ask students to find and point to the expressions and words on the board in the text of the song.
- Read the song aloud. Have students repeat.
- Play CS20. Have students listen and read.
- Play CS20 again. Have students join in the song.

Practice (STUDENT BOOK p.31)

8. Sentence completion: Ask students to make sentences starting *I'd like to ...* Write a list of useful verbs on the board: *go, play, talk to, have, meet.*

Reading and writing (WORKBOOK p.30)

9. **Activity ②** Have students read the story in their Student Book again and answer the questions.

Answers   1. a hat   2. Spider Smith   3. in Australia
               4. the Book of Adabra and the missing pages.
               5. She didn't like him.

10. **Activity ③** Have students draw lines through the maze to find out where the people want to go. Then have them write sentences.

Answers   1. "I'd like to go to Australia."
               2. "I'd like to go to Brazil."
               3. "I'd like to go to China."
               4. "I'd like to go to Greece."
               5. "I'd like to go to Mars."

UNIT 8

Ending the lesson

11. Sing *I'd like to teach the world to sing* again.

Lesson Three

Language focus
Review: Past simple.

New words
actor   became (past tense)   for example
framed (= incriminated)   liked (past tense)   popular
science fiction   sound (noun)   special effects

Review/Warm-up

1. Review *would like to*. Write the following scrambled sentences on the board.
   1. hat. this wear to like I like 'd (I'd like to wear this hat.)
   2. on? you put that to Would coat like (Would you like to put that coat on?)
   3. tea, I some like green please 'd (I'd like some green tea, please).
- Pair work: Have students work together to put the sentences in the right order. Then ask students to tell you who said each sentence.

Answers   1. Ken   2. Lucky Lorenz   3. Uncle John

2. Sing the song *I'd like to teach the world to sing* again.

Reading (STUDENT BOOK p.32)

3. *Hollywood.* Before reading: Books closed: Ask students to tell you all the words they know already about movie making: *movie director, studio, camera, cameraman, movie theater,* etc. Write these words on the board. Ask: *What kind of movie did the children see at the movie studio? (a cowboy movie). Did the cowboys have real guns? (no). Were they real cowboys? (no).* Say: *They were actors.* Write the word *actor* on the board. Pre-teach *science fiction.* Ask students to tell you the names of movies that they like. Write the categories *adventure, love story, cartoon, science fiction* on the board. Ask students to say which category their favorite movies fall into. Add *comedy* and *musical* (which do not appear in the Student Book) if necessary. Pre-teach *sound* and *special effects* by translation.
- Write focus questions on the board:
   a. What can you visit in Hollywood? (the movie studios).
   b. Did movies in the 1900s have sound? (no)
   c. Do directors use special effects in science fiction movies? (yes)

4. Books open: Say: *Can you see the word "Hollywood" in the first picture? Point to a black and white movie. Point to an actor. Point to a cartoon.* Students point.
- Scanning: Write on the board: *California, adventures, cowboy movies, cartoons, science fiction, special effects.* Have students find and point to these words in the text.
- Have students read the passage silently and answer the questions on the board.
- Ask students to guess the meanings of *popular* and *for example.* Translate framed (incriminated) in *Who Framed Roger Rabbit?* if students ask what it means.
- Pair work: Have students read the passage again and answer the questions in the book.

Answers   1. in California, in the United States
2. No, they didn't.
3. in the 1920s
4. cowboy movies
5. cartoons and science fiction

5. Write the following headings on the board:
the 1900s   the 1920s   now
Then read aloud the following: *the first movies, many different kinds of movies, black and white movies, "talking" movies, no sound, cowboy movies, special effects.* As you read each one, select students to come to the board and write them under the correct heading.

Reading and writing (WORKBOOK pp. 31–32)

6. WB p.31 **Activity** ④ Have students look at the pictures and complete the sentences under the pictures.

Answers   2. Would you like to wear this blouse?/No, thank you, it's too small.
3. Would you like to wear this hat?/No, thank you, it's too big.
4. Would you like to wear these magic sun glasses?

7. **Activity** ⑤ Spelling: Have students complete the words.

Answers   1. night   2. eighty   3. eight   4. ghost
5. knife   6. knock   7. knee

8. WB p.32 **Activity** ⑥ Have students read the descriptions of the movies and write the letters in the boxes.

Answers   1. B   2. D   3. A   4. C

9. Activity ⑦ Have students answer the questions about the movies.

Answers 1. A and B   2. C   3. A and D (C also has the cowboys' horses)   4. A

Ending the lesson

10. Dictation: Dictate the following passage. Read each section twice, slowly.
Hollywood is/the movie center/of the world./Directors make/many different kinds of movies./The most popular movies now/are cartoons/and science fiction movies.

11. Sing either *Home on the range* or *I'd like to teach the world to sing.*

Be prepared!

Make sets of cards offering alternatives: *tea/coffee; train/bus; tennis/basketball.*
- Prepare Yes/No coins (one for each pair of students) and counters (one for each student).

UNIT 9

Lesson One

Language focus
Future simple: *Will you ...? Yes, I will./No, I won't.*

New words
explore   crocodile   footprint   hole   mountains   rock
sand   shark   swim (noun)   treasure   will   won't

Review/Warm-up

1. Sing *I'd like to teach the world to sing* (CS20).

2. Review geographical expressions: *island, sea, land, trees, hills, cave, road, north, south, east, west.* Draw a simple plan of an island on the board, without labels. Have students come up to the board and label the features. When the map is finished, point out that the hills are very big. Say: *These aren't hills. They're bigger. They are mountains.* Write *mountains* on the board.

Presentation (STUDENT BOOK p.33)

3. A game: "Explore Treasure Island." Pre-teach *will*: Put a pair of prepared cards of alternatives, e.g., *tea* and *coffee*, face down on a table. Say: *[George], pick up a card, please. Will you have [tea]? (Yes/No) Yes, I will./No, I won't.* Repeat the process with another pair of cards, e.g., *train* and *bus*. Say: *[Maria] Will you go by [bus]? (Yes, I will./No, I won't).*
Write: *Will you ...? Yes, I will./No, I won't* on the board.
- Pre-teach *explore* and *treasure* by translation.
- Books open. Pre-teach *crocodile, footprint, hole, rock, sand, shark* by reference to the picture. Say: *Point to the treasure. Point to the sharks. Point to the footprints. Point to the mountains. Point to the crocodile,* etc. Have students find the things in the picture, point to them and repeat.

UNIT 9

4. Play the game: Pair work: Give each pair a Yes/No coin and two counters. Say: *Point to the boat. This is where you start. Then follow the "This Way" sign.* Every time students reach a question, they must stop and both players flip the coin, one after the other. Students follow either the "yes" or "no" road until they get to the next question. When they reach an obstacle, such as the sharks, they have to go back to the previous question.
- Explain the game briefly. When students start playing, go around the class helping them, and making sure they understand the rules. The first student to find the treasure is the winner.

Practice (STUDENT BOOK p.33)

5. Books open: Have students look at the map of the island again. Point to the first crossroads. Then tell students: *I'm here. I'm turning left. Will I go for a swim?* Students answer: *Yes, you will.* Continue around the island in the same way.

6. Postcards: Pair work: Ask students to draw and write postcards from Treasure Island. They should write about some of the things that happened to them, in the past simple tense. To prepare for this, write the relevant verbs on the board: *go for a swim, chase, find, see, hide, fall down*. Ask students to write the past tense forms next to these.

Reading and writing (WORKBOOK p.33)

7. Activity ① Have students write sentences with *will*. Have students find the answers in the crystal ball.

Answers
1. You'll win an important game or quiz.
2. You'll meet a dinosaur in the street near your house.
3. You'll find a big spider in your bed or in your shoes.
4. You'll go to sleep in a math lesson at school.
5. You'll forget to go to a friend's birthday party.
6. You'll buy some purple socks.
7. You'll see a ghost outside the window one night.
8. You'll fall off your bicycle or skateboard.

- Have students use the crystal ball to ask and answer questions about each other: *What will you do next week? I'll ...*

Ending the lesson

8. (Extra) Group work: Have students draw their own treasure islands. They should include different geographical features, but they should not show where the treasure is buried. Then have them challenge students from other groups to find their treasure. Students ask: *Will I find the treasure near the mountains?* The other student answers: *Yes, you will./No, you won't.*

Lesson Two

Language focus
Future simple: *I'll go ..., Will he ...? Yes, he will./No, he won't.*

New words
angrily   anything   in the middle of   knock present (= gift)   quicker   ship   shut up!   stupid take (train, etc.)   *whispered* (past tense)

Review/Warm-up

1. Ask questions about Treasure Island: *[George], did the sharks chase you? (Yes, they did./No, they didn't.)*, etc.

Story presentation (STUDENT BOOK p.34, CS21)

2. *Ringo Dingo.* The story so far: Lucky Lorenz told Uncle John that Spider Smith is also looking for the missing pages from the Book of Adabra. Spider Smith is now in Australia with his friend, Ringo Dingo.
- Before listening: Ask questions about the story so far: *Somebody else is looking for the missing pages. Who is it? (Spider Smith) Where is Spider Smith now? (in Australia) Who is Ringo Dingo? (Spider's friend) Is Ringo Dingo dangerous? (Yes, he is.)*
- Prediction: Ask students to predict what will happen next in the story: *Will Uncle John meet Spider Smith? Will Spider Smith find the missing pages? Will Uncle John and the children go to Australia?* Tell students that they will find the right answers to these questions when they read the story.
- Pre-teach *in the middle of*. Place an object in the center of a table top. Say: *My pencil is in the middle of the table. [Maria], please go and stand in the middle of the table. [Maria], please go and stand in the middle of the room.* Ask: *What's in the middle of Treasure Island? (the mountains)*

- Before listening: Write focus questions on the board.
  a. Where is Ringo Dingo's house? (in the middle of Australia)
  b. Where do Uncle John and the children hide? (behind some rocks)
  c. What's in the box? (a shopping list)

3. Books open. Play CS21. Have students listen and read.
- Play CS21 again. Have students listen, read and then answer the focus questions.
- After listening: Ask students to guess from the context the meanings of *angrily, anything, shut up!, stupid,* and *whispered.*

Story practice

4. Ask students further questions about the story: *What kind of animals did Kate see? (sheep). Who did they see with Ringo Dingo? (Spider Smith). What did Ringo and Spider have? (a box). Who stole the box? (Ringo). Who did he steal it from? (Kashoki). Did Ringo Dingo learn anything about the missing pages? (no) Were the missing pages in the box? (no). Why didn't Kashoki tell Ringo Dingo about the missing pages? (Because Kashoki didn't like Ringo Dingo). Who is going to go to Japan? (Spider Smith).*

5. Dialogue: Give students a list of the speakers and ask them to write in the lines of dialogue from the story.

Kate:

Ken:

Uncle John:

Caroline:

Uncle John:

Ken:

Ringo Dingo:

Spider:

Ringo Dingo:

Spider:

Ringo Dingo:

Spider:

Ringo Dingo:

Spider:

- Have students act out the dialogue in groups. Have one or two groups act it out for the whole class.

6. Write the following half sentences on the board, in random order: *Uncle John whispered/because he didn't want Spider and Ringo to hear him. Ringo was angry/because Spider didn't find the Book of Adabra in America. Spider was angry/because Ringo didn't learn anything about the missing pages. Spider has to go to Japan/because he wants to talk to Kashoki.* Have students draw lines matching the sentence halves.

Presentation (STUDENT BOOK p.35, CS22)

7. *What is Spider thinking?* Pre-teach *knock, present, ship* (a big boat), *quicker.* Ask: *Is a ship quicker than a plane?* Draw a ship and a present on the board. Demonstrate *knock* on the classroom door. Write the new words on the board. Have students read out loud.

8. Scanning. Books open: Have students point to the new words in the text. Read the sentences out loud. Ask students to guess the meaning of *take a train* from the context.
- Read and match: Have students match the sentences and the pictures.

Answers   A. Then I'll buy a nice present for Kashoki ... a plastic spider.
B. I'll knock on Kashoki's door and I'll give him the present.
C. No, I think I'll fly. It's quicker.
D. I'll get some Japanese money at Tokyo airport.
E. Maybe I'll go to Japan by ship.
F. I'll take the bus from the airport to Kashoki's house.

- Play CS22. Have students listen.
- Play CS22 again. Have students listen and answer.

Tapescript

Answers
Voice 1:   Listen and answer: *Yes, he will* or *No, he won't.*
Voice 2:   Will Spider go to Japan by car?
   (Students answer: *No, he won't.*)
   Will Spider buy some Greek money at Tokyo airport?
   (Students answer: *No, he won't.*)
   Will Spider buy a present for Kashoki?
   (Students answer: *Yes, he will.*)
   Will Spider buy a bird made of paper for Kashoki?
   (Students answer: *No, he won't.*)
   Will Spider take the bus from the airport to Kashok'si house?
   (Students answer: *Yes, he will.*)

UNIT 9

Practice (STUDENT BOOK p.35)

9. Write the following paragraph on the board. Have students fill in the blanks.

Spider will ... to Japan. He'll get some ... at Tokyo ... Then he'll ... a plastic... for ... He'll ... a bus from the ... to ... He'll ... on Kashoki's ... and he'll ... him the ...

Reading and writing (WORKBOOK p.34)

10. **Activity ②** Have students read the story in their Student Book again, and then write questions for the answers.

Answers
1. Where were Uncle John and the children?
2. Who was Spider Smith with?
3. Who did Ringo steal the box from?
4. What was inside the box?
5. What must Spider do?/Who must Spider talk to?

11. **Activity ③** Have students match the pictures and then write the words spoken by the children.

Answers
2. "I'll bring the beach umbrella."
3. "I'll bring the beach ball."
4. "I'll bring the cookies."
5. "I'll bring the cassettes."
5. "I'll bring the hippo."

Ending the lesson

12. Sing *I'd like to teach the world to sing* again.

Lesson Three

Language focus
Review: Present simple, Expressing ability: *can*.

New words
Aborigine continent desert dingo high kangaroo koala outback pocket pouch sharp wool

Review/Warm-up

1. Review *will*. Say: *We're going to go to [the beach] tomorrow. Maybe I'll [go for a swim]. What will you do, [George]?* Have students continue making suggestions, using the pattern: *Maybe I'll ...*

Reading (STUDENT BOOK p.36)

2. *Australia.* Before reading: Pre-teach *continent* by referring to the map of the world on SB p.3. Pre-teach *pocket, sharp,* and *wool* by translation, and *high* by demonstration. Write these new words on the board.

- Books open: Pre-teach: *Aborigine, desert, dingo, kangaroo, pouch, koala* by referring to the pictures. Write these new words on the board.
- Scanning: Ask students to find the new words, listed on the board, in the text.
- Write focus questions on the board:
  a. How many people live in Australia? (seventeen million)
  b. What changes color under the sun? (Ayers Rock)
  c. Which Australian animals can jump very high? (kangaroos)

3. Have students either read on their own or work in pairs. Go around the class helping students to work out the meaning of the passage. Have students answer the questions on the board.

- Ask students to guess the meaning of *outback* from the context. Explain that this is an Australian word that is not used to describe deserts in other parts of the world.

4. Answer the questions: Read aloud the six questions. Have students tell you the answers.

Answers
1. Because many of their families came from England two hundred years ago.
2. No. It is usually hot and dry.
3. In the middle of the outback.
4. Sheep and crocodiles.
5. Dingos, kangaroos, and koalas.
6. They keep their babies in pouches.

Reading and writing (WORKBOOK pp.35–36)

5. WB p.35 **Activity ④** Have students choose the verbs and adverbs to complete the sentences. Do examples together orally first.

Answers
1. Mr. Jones is painting carelessly.
2. Mrs. Jones is shouting angrily.
3. Jane is whispering quietly.
4. John is laughing happily.

6. **Activity ⑤** Have students fill in the blanks in the sentences, using the words in the box.

Answers island, saw, teeth, than, chased, quickly, climbed, frightened, left, found, found, looked

7. **WB p.36 Activity ⑥** Have students complete the crossword puzzle. Remind students that all the questions are about Australia.

Answers

		¹B	A	B	I	E	S		
	²C	O	U	N	T	R	Y		
			³S	H	E	E	P		
⁴C	O	N	T	I	N	E	N	T	S
⁵A	B	O	R	I	G	I	N	E	S
⁶K	A	N	G	A	R	O	O	S	
⁷K	O	A	L	A	S				
⁸E	N	G	L	I	S	H			
⁹O	U	T	B	A	C	K			

The country is Australia.

Ending the lesson

8. (Extra) Project: Have students make a wall display about Australia, including drawings and pictures from magazines, if possible.

9. Spelling: Dictate the following words for students to write down: 1. continent 2. kangaroo 3. crocodile 4. frightening 5. pouch 6. special 7. million 8. desert 9. weather 10. famous

Be prepared!

Bring to the next class a soft bag and various small objects, e.g., an apple, a ball, a coin, a button, a stone.

UNIT 10

Lesson One

Language focus
Comparing objects: *Looks like ... /sounds like ...*

New words
feel (verb) *like* (= similar) *sound* (verb)

Review/Warm-up

1. Introduce: *What ... like?* Say: *What's the weather like today? It's [hot]. What's [Maria] like? She's tall.* Have students repeat. Review the reading passage about Australia. Ask: *What is the weather in Australia like?* (hot and dry) *What are Australian farms like?* (very big) *What are crocodiles's teeth like?* (very sharp) *What are kangaroos' legs like?* (very strong).

Presentation (STUDENT BOOK p.37, CS23)

2. *Looks like, sounds like ...* Pre-teach *looks/sounds/feels like ...* Say: *Look at the picture of a dingo. It looks like a dog.* Write on the board: *A dingo looks like a dog.* Draw a picture of a cat on the board. Ask: *Does this picture look like a sheep? Does it look like a rabbit? What does it look like?* (*It looks like a cat.*) Make animal sounds. Ask: *What did that sound like?* Have students take turns making animal noises, and asking and answering questions. Say: *[George], close your eyes.* Give the student an object, e.g., an apple. Ask: *What does it feel like, [George]? Does it feel like a box? Does it feel like an orange?*

3. Listen and read: Play CS23. Have students listen and read.

Tapescript

Voice 1:	Listen and read.
Boy:	What is it?
Girl 1:	I don't know ...
Girl 2:	It looks like a statue.
Girl 1:	It feels like ice cream. It's very cold.
Boy:	Brrr!
Ghost:	Woooahhh!
Girl 2:	It sounds like a ghost.
All:	Aagh! It is a ghost!

- Ask: *What does the ghost look like?* (a statue). *What does if feel like?* (ice cream). *What does it sound like?* (a ghost).

UNIT 10

4. Ask and answer: Pair work: Practice the first question and answer with the whole class: *What does picture A look like? (It looks like a toothbrush.)* Have students work in pairs, asking and answering questions about the other objects. Check answers with the whole class.

Answers A. a toothbrush   B. a roller skate
C. a paintbrush   D. a mouse   E. a tree   F. a train

Practice (STUDENT BOOK p.37, CS24)

5. Before listening: Point to the pictures. Ask: *What's this? (It's a chimpanzee),* etc.
- Play CS24. Have students listen and point.

Tapescript

Answers
Voice 1:   Listen and point.
　　　　　One.　(Students point to the chimpanzee.)
　　　　　Two.　(Students point to the robot.)
　　　　　Three.　(Students point to the dog.)
　　　　　Four.　(Students point to the bird.)
　　　　　Five.　(Students point to the airplane.)
　　　　　Six.　(Students point to the frog.)

- Practice the first question and answer with the whole class. *What does number 1 sound like? (It sounds like a chimpanzee.)*
- Play CS24 again. Have students listen and say the answers out loud.

6. Practice *It feels like ...* Without letting students see, put a small object in a bag. Say: *What's in the bag?* Let a student feel the bag. Ask: *What does it feel like? (It feels like [an apple].)* Then say: *You're right. It's an apple. Try again.* Repeat the process with different objects.

Reading and writing (WORKBOOK p.37)

7. Activity ① Have students look at the shapes and make sentences, saying what the shapes look like. Do one or two examples orally. Then have students write the answers.

Answers
2. This looks like a tree.
3. This looks like a bird.
4. This looks like a spider.
5. This looks like a hand.
6. This looks like a crocodile.

8. Activity ② this is similar to Activity 1. Have students look at the pictures and decide what the people look like. Then have them write sentences.

Answers
1. She looks like an elephant.
2. She looks like a cat.
3. He looks like a lion.
4. She looks like a fish.
5. He looks like a monkey.

Ending the lesson

9. Animals sounds: Ask students to make animal sounds. Other students have to guess what the animal is.

Lesson Two

Language focus
Regular and irregular plurals.

New words
across   boxes   feet   get to   knife   mice   women

Review/Warm-up

1. Guessing game: Review *sounds like ...* Divide the class into two teams. Say: *I'm thinking of a color. It sounds like bed.* The first team to shout out *red* scores a point. Continue asking with: *an animal/house (mouse); something in the sky/car (star); a number/blue (two); something to wear/bat (hat); something to wear/box (socks); an animal/dog (frog); something to eat/snake (cake); an animal/fat (cat); a number/pen (ten).*

Story presentation (STUDENT BOOK p.38, CS25)

2. *Crocodiles!* The story so far: Uncle John and the children are in Australia. They overheard Spider Smith and Ringo Dingo talking. Spider Smith is going to Japan to talk to Kashoki about the missing pages from the Book of Adabra.

- Before listening: Ask questions about the story so far: *Where are Uncle John and the children now? (in Australia). Who did they see in Australia? (Spider Smith and Ringo Dingo). Who is Spider going to talk to? (Kashoki) Where does Kashoki live? (in Japan).*
- Ask students to predict what will happen next: *Will Spider Smith go to Japan? Will Kashoki tell him about the missing pages? Will Uncle John and the children go to Japan?*
- Write focus questions on the board:
　a. Why must they go to Japan quickly? (Because they must talk to Kashoki before Spider Smith gets there.)
　b. What chased Uncle John and the children? (Ringo's dog)
　c. What were under the bridge? (crocodiles)
　d. Who did Uncle John and Barker attack? (Ringo)
　e. Where did they put Ringo? (in the kangaroo cage)

- Books open: Play CS25. Have students listen and read.
- Play CS25 again. Have students listen and answer the focus questions.
- After listening: Ask students to guess the meaning of *get to* and *across* from the context.

Story practice

3. Ask further questions about the story: *Where did Ringo Dingo hide? (behind a rock) Where did Ringo's dog chase Uncle John and the children? (across the bridge) What happened next? (The bridge opened and they fell through.) What did the crocodiles do? (They opened their mouths.) Why did all the crocodiles have magic wands in their mouths? (Because Uncle John said a spell.) Who looked like a kangaroo? (Ringo).*

4. Dialogue: Group work: Give students the following lines of dialogue and ask them to arrange them in the order in which they appear in the story, together with the names of the speakers.

_____: 98, 99, 100 ... SHAZAM!
_____: That was VERY interesting.
_____: Put him in the kangaroo cage.
_____: Kashoki knows about the missing pages. But he didn't tell Ringo.
_____: We must go to Japan quickly. We must talk to Kashoki before Spider gets there. Come on. Let's go.
_____: Whew! They can't eat us now!
_____: Turn around, John Jones! Well, well! You want the missing pages from the Book of Adabra. But you're not going to get them!
_____: What are we going to do with Ringo?
_____: He IS a criminal. He's a very bad man. But don't worry. He can't chase us now. And we're going to Japan! We must talk to Kashoki before Spider ...
_____: You can't stop us, Ringo Dingo.
_____: Right! Then we must go back to the Time Machine quickly.
_____: Oh, can't I? Go on, across the bridge. Here are some new friends for you!
_____: He looks like a kangaroo.
_____: Help! Uncle John!
_____: He looks like a criminal.

- Have students practice the dialogue in groups. Have one or two groups act out the dialogue for the class.

5. Sequencing: Pair work: Write the following events from the story on the board. Have students rewrite them in the order in which they happened in the story.

a. They put Ringo Dingo in a kangaroo cage.
b. Suddenly all the crocodiles had magic wands in their mouths.
c. They went away in the Time Machine.
d. Uncle John said his fastest spell.
e. Everybody climbed out of the hole.

Presentation (STUDENT BOOK p.39, CS26)

6. *More than one...*Books open. Look and say: Read out loud: *One apple, two apples,* etc. Pay special attention to the pronunciation of *boxes* and the new word, *knife* and its plural, *knives*.

7. Listen and repeat: Before listening. Pre-teach new words: *feet, mice,* and *women* by referring students to the pictures.
- Scanning: On the board, write the singular forms: man, child, mouse, foot, woman, sheep, baby, tooth. Have students find the plurals of these words in the rhyme. Ask students to write the plurals on the board.
- Play CS26. Have students listen and repeat.
- Play CS26 again. Have students listen and point to the pictures.

Tapescript

Voice 1: Listen and repeat.
Voice 2: One man is selling hats.
Two men are painting cats.
Three women are making flowers.
Four children are counting hours.
Five sheep have dirty feet.
Six babies have clean teeth.
Seven boxes are full of rocks.
Eight mice are wearing socks.
One, two, three, four, five, six, seven, eight,
Writing poems is really great.

Practice (STUDENT BOOK p.39)

8. Books closed. Practice irregular plurals: Erase the plurals from the board. Ask students to come to the board and write them.
- Play CS26 again. Have students listen and repeat.

Reading and writing (WORKBOOK p.38)

9. Activity ③ Reference: Have students read the sentences and refer to the story on SB pp.38–39 for help in answering the questions.

Answers 1. Japan 2. the missing pages
3. Uncle John and the children 4. the bridge 5. Ringo Dingo

UNIT 10

10. **Activity** ④ Alphabet quiz. Have students answer these questions as quickly as possible. Time them as they do the questions. Tell them when to start and ask them to raise their hands as soon as they finish.

Answers 2. b 3. c 4. c 5. a 6. b 7. a

11. **Activity** ⑤ Spelling: Have students write the words for the pictures.

Answers building, fruit, dinosaur, astronaut, turtle, nurse, music, magic

Ending the lesson

12. Spelling: Read aloud the following words. Have students write them down. 1. *boxes* 2. *knives* 3. *babies* 4. *children* 5. *feet* 6. *mice* 7. *women* 8. *sheep* Check spellings.
- Have students write the singular forms of the words on the list.

13. (Extra) Writing and drawing: Have students write the poem, substituting pictures for words.

Lesson Three

New words
absolutely crunch (verb) *enormous fishes
keep* (= maintain) *lose* (verb) *sharpest smile* (noun)
suitable supper

Review/Warm-up

1. Review irregular plurals: Play CS26 again. Have students listen and repeat.

Song presentation (STUDENT BOOK p.40, CS27)

2. *The shark and the tiger and the crocodile.* Books open. Talk about the pictures: Say: *Point to the shark. Point to the crocodile. Point to the tiger.* Students point. Ask: *What's the crocodile doing? (He's brushing his teeth.) Are the tiger's teeth clean? (Yes)* Pre-teach *keep*. Say: *The crocodile keeps his teeth clean.* Ask: *Does the shark keep his teeth clean? Do you keep your teeth clean? Do you keep your shoes clean?*

3. Pre-teach *supper*. Explain that this is a meal eaten in the evening, although both can be used to describe the meal eaten after work or school. Pre-teach *enormous*. Say: *An elephant is a very big animal. It is enormous!* Pre-teach *crunch, absolutely,* and *suitable* by translation.
- Write focus questions on the board:
  a. What are the crocodile's teeth like? (clean and beautiful)
  b. What do the shark, the tiger and the crocodile never lose? (their smile)
  c. Which animal's teeth are the sharpest in the sea? (the white shark's)
  d. Which animal has enormous teeth? (the tiger)
- Play CS 27. Have students listen and read.
- Play CS 27 again. Have students listen and answer the focus questions.
- Play CS27 again. Have students sing along with the tape.
- Ask further questions about the song: *When does the tiger eat his supper? (at night) Which animal has teeth that crunch? (the crocodile) Which animal has teeth that bite? (the tiger).*

Reading and writing (WORKBOOK pp.39–40)

4. WB p.39 **Activity** ⑥ Writing: Work together as a class. Write the sentences (in the past simple tense) on the board.

Answers Ringo Dingo and Spider Smith were in the jungle, in Africa. They were near a river, under a tree. Ringo sat on a rock. He opened his water bottle and started to have a drink. Spider shouted, "Look! It looks like a crocodile! We must leave quickly!" Suddenly the rock started to move. Ringo looked at it. It had small eyes! But it had a big mouth! The crocodile turned its head and it opened its mouth. Spider and Ringo were up in a tall tree. The crocodile went for a swim in the river.

5. WB p.40 **Activity** ⑦ Reading: Have students read the passage and answer the questions.

Answers 1. about eighteen meters
2. with their noses
3. Because they have very strong tails.
4. other, smaller fish
5. Because they sometimes attack people.

Ending the lesson

6. Sing *The shark and the tiger and the crocodile* again.

Testing

Now is an appropriate time to test students on the previous five units.

These suggestions are intended to complement the reading and writing test exercises in *American Chatterbox* Tests at the end of this Teacher's Book.
- Spelling: Read aloud the following ten words for students to write and spell.

  1. fantastic   2. happiest   3. popular   4. ghost
  5. knock   6. knives   7. build   8. bought
  9. inch   10. thinnest

- Dictation: Read aloud each section of the following dictation twice. Have students listen and write.

The heaviest land animal in the world/is the African elephant./It weighs more than 2½ tons.

Read through the whole dictation again for students to listen and check.

- Composition: Ask students to write four or five sentences about Australia.

- Oral assessment: Use the pictures on SB p.25. Ask students about Wizzo's diary: *What did Wizzo do last Friday? What's he going to do next Friday?*, etc.

UNIT 11

Lesson One

Language focus
Talking about money.
Talking about prices: *How much ...?*

New words
coin   dime   half dollar bill   how much?   nickel   penny
quarter   round (= circular)   side   use (verb)

Review/Warm-up

1. Sing *The shark and the tiger and the crocodile* (CS27) again.

2. Review *How many ...?* and *There are ...* Ask: *How many days are there in a week? How many months are there in a year? How many minutes are there in an hour?*

Presentation (STUDENT BOOK p.41, CS28)

3. *Money.* Books open. Before listening: Ask: *What can you see in the pictures? (money).* Pre-teach *penny* and review *dollar.* Explain that this is American money. Pre-teach *coin* and *bill* using examples of your national currency.
- Pre-teach *round* by demonstration: draw a circle on the board. Ask students to show you other round objects in the classroom.
- Scanning: Write the foillowing on the board: *penny, nickel, dime, quarter, ten dollar bill.* Ask students to find and point to these in the passage.
- Write focus questions on the board:
  a. What money do people use in the United States? (dollars and cents)
  b. How many cents are there in a dollar? (one hundred)
  c. Which is the smallest coin? (the ten cent dime)
  d. What are the coins made of? (metal)
- Play CS 28. Have students listen and read.
- Play CS 28 again. Have students listen and answer the focus questions.

Tapescript

Voice 1:   Listen and read.
Voice 2:   What money do people use in your country? In the United States people use dollars and cents. There are one hundred cents in a dollar.

UNIT 11

American coins are round. The smallest coin is the dime. There are ten cents in a dime. The biggest coin is the silver dollar. There are not many silver dollars. People often keep them because they are special.
The other coins are the one cent penny, the five cent nickel, the twenty-five cent quarter, and the fifty cent half dollar. The coins are made of metal, but the five and ten dollar bills are made of paper.

4. Identify the money: Ask: *Which is the smallest coin? (the dime) Which coin is the biggest? (the silver dollar).* Point to the silver dollar. Students point.

Practice (STUDENT BOOK p.41, CS29)

5. Listen and point: Before listening: Books open. Say: *Point to the basketball. Point to the calendar. Point to the book about planets. Point to the tiger. Point to the bag of marbles. Point to the box of paints. Point to the stamp album.* Students point.
- Practice the question and answer: *How much is the skateboard?* with the whole class.
- Play CS29. Have students listen and point.

Tapescript

Voice 1: Listen and point.
Voice 2: How much is the skateboard?
Voice 3: It's forty-five dollars.
Voice 2: How much is the book about planets?
Voice 3: It's ten dollars.
Voice 2: How much is the basketball?
Voice 3: It's twelve dollars and fifty cents.
Voice 2: How much is the calendar?
Voice 3: It's six dollars.
Voice 2: How much is the tiger?
Voice 3: It's nine dollars.
Voice 2: How much is the bag of marbles?
Voice 3: It's two dollars.
Voice 2: How much is the stamp album?
Voice 3: It's five dollars and seventy cents.
Voice 2: How much is the box of paints?
Voice 3: It's four dollars and sixty cents.

6. Pair work: Have students ask and answer about the prices of all the items on the page.

7. Extend the dialogue:
   A: Can I help you?
   B: Yes. I'd like a [bag of marbles]. How much is it?
   A: It's two dollars.

Reading and writing (WORKBOOK p.41)

8. **Activity ①** Have students complete the sentences with the information from the pictures.

Answers 1. They're $6.80. 2. It's $12.20. 3. How much is the calculator? 4. How much is the hippo? 5. How much are the roller skates? 6. How much is the soccer ball?

Ending the lesson

9. Writing: Have students write about their own money. Use a similar pattern to the passage on SB p.41: *In ... people use ... There are ... in one ... The smallest coin is the ... coin. The biggest coin is the ... coin.*

10. (Extra) Project: Foreign coins. Have students bring foreign coins to class and make a display, labeling coins with their country of origin and denomination.

Lesson Two

Language focus
Future intentions: *I'll buy ...*

New words
everything   far   flew   guitar   Italian   or
sat (past tense)   toy

Review/Warm-up

1. Review *How much ...?* by asking questions about the items on SB p.41.

Story presentation (STUDENT BOOK p.42, CS30)

2. *A friend in Japan.* The story so far: Spider Smith went to Japan to try to find out from Kashoki, the Japanese magician, about the missing pages from the Book of Adabra. Uncle John and the children escaped from Ringo Dingo in Australia and are going to Japan in the Time Machine.
- Before listening: Books closed. Ask questions about the story so far: *Where did Spider Smith go? (to Japan) Who does he want to see? (Kashoki) Where are Uncle John and the children going? (to Japan).*
- Predicting: Ask students: *Who will Uncle John see in Japan? Will he meet Spider Smith again? What will Uncle John ask about?*
- Write focus questions on the board:
   a. Who does Uncle John phone?   (Lucky Lorenz)
   b. Do they take a train to Kashoki's house?   (No, they don't. They walk.)
   c. Do they see Spider Smith?   (no)

d. Does Kashoki like Uncle John? (yes)
e. Does he tell Uncle John about the Book of Adabra? (yes)
- Books open. Play CS30. Have students listen and read.
- Play CS30 again. Have students listen and answer the focus questions.
- Ask students to guess the meanings of *everything, far, flew,* and *sat* from the context.

Story practice

3. Books open. Ask further questions about the story: *What did Lucky Lorenz tell Uncle John? (Kashoki's address). What did they buy for Kashoki? (a present, a paper bird full of chocolate). How did they go to Kashoki's house? (They walked through a park.) Was Spider Smith in the park? (yes). Where was Spider Smith? (up in a tree). What did Uncle John show Kashoki? (the Book of Adabra). Where are the missing pages? (in Egypt). What did Kashoki give Uncle John? (a map of the pyramid of Queen Neops). Where must Uncle John and the children go next? (to Egypt). How will they go? (in the Time Machine).*

4. Dialogue: Group work: Give students the script of the following dialogue, with blanks. Have students complete the dialogue of the phone call between Spider Smith and Ringo Dingo.

Spider: Hello. Ringo?
Ringo: Spider! Where are you?
Spider: I'm in ...
Ringo: Did you talk to Kashoki?
Spider: ... But John Jones talked to him. Kashoki told John Jones about ... ...
Ringo: Where are the missing pages?
Spider: ... ...
Ringo: You must go to ... quickly.
Spider: But I don't have a ... ...
Ringo: Oh no. How can you go?
Spider: I have an idea.

- Have students practice the dialogue in pairs.
- Have one or two pairs act out the story in front of the class.

Presentation (STUDENT BOOK p.43, CS31)

5. *Presents from different countries.* Before listening: Books open. Pre-teach *Italian, guitar,* and *toy.* Point to the guitar. Say: *This is a guitar. Is it from Italy? (no). It's not Italian. Is it a toy guitar or a real guitar?*

- Listen and point. Play CS31. Have students listen.
- Play CS31 again. Have students listen and point.

Tapescript

Voice 1: Listen and point to the presents.
Voice 2: Here's a Chinese bowl.
Here's a Greek bag.
Look at this Italian vase.
I like this American T-shirt.
Here's some Egyptian jewelry
I like this Japanese doll.
Look at this Spanish guitar.
Here's an Australian toy kangaroo.

- Ask questions about the pictures: *Is this a Greek vase? (No, it's an Italian vase),* etc.

Practice (STUDENT BOOK p.43)

6. Choose presents for the family. Practice the conversation on SB p.43: *(What will you buy for your family?,* etc.) with the whole class.
- Ask and answer: Pair work: Explain that students can choose things from this page and from SB p.41. Have students take turns asking and answering.

Reading and writing (WORKBOOK p.42)

7. **Activity** ② Have students read the story in the Student Book again, and use it to make sentences for the words.

Answers
1. Uncle John and the children went to Japan in the Time Machine.
2. They walked to Kashoki's house through a Japanese park.
3. Spider Smith was up in a tree in the park.
4. Uncle John showed Kashoki the Book of Adabra.
5. Kashoki told them to go backward in time to 2500 B.C.

8. **Activity** ③ Have students write their own and their friends' addresses in the same way as the example address. Work with students to write an example address on the board first.

Ending the lesson

9. Role play: Shopping. Group work: Have students draw a store window full of presents. They ask and answer: *What will you buy for your [sister]?,* etc.

UNIT 11

Lesson Three

Language focus
Review: Present simple.

New words
a lot of   also   colored   fold (verb)   *mat   modern motorcycle   radio   hobby   origami*

Review/Warm-up

1. Review *How much?* Use the pictures on SB p.41 as a basis for the dialogue: *I went shopping yesterday/What did you buy?/I bought .../How much was it?/$ ...*

Reading (STUDENT BOOK p.44)

2. *Japan.* Books open. Before reading: Pre-teach *fold* by demonstration. Pre-teach *colored, mat, motorcycle, modern, radio,* and *hobby* by translation. Pre-teach *origami* by referring to the picture.
- Point to the pictures: Say: *Point to a computer. Point to a modern building. Point to an old Japanese house.* Students point. Ask: *What is the Japanese child doing? (origami/folding paper).*
- Write focus questions on the board:
  a. Is Tokyo a modern city? (yes)
  b. What are the walls and doors inside an old Japanese house made of? (paper)
  c. What do Japanese children love to watch on television? (modern cartoons)
- Reading: Have students read alone, silently. Go around the class helping them.
- Pair work: Have students work out the answers to the focus questions on the board in pairs.
- After reading: Read aloud the questions on SB p.44. Have students listen and repeat the questions. Ask the questions again. Have students answer. Then have students answer in pairs.
- Have students write the answers out as sentences. Help them where necessary.

Answers
1. Japan is rich because it makes and sells many of our modern machines.
2. The capital city of Japan is Tokyo.
3. Old Japanese houses are made of wood.
4. People sit on mats.
5. They make animals and birds.

3. Ask further questions: *What kinds of modern machines do they make in Japan? (cars, motorcycles, computers, televisions, and radios) Are there a lot of factories in Tokyo? (yes) Are there any chairs or beds inside the old houses? (no) What kind of tables do people eat at? (small tables) Is origami a very old hobby? (yes).*

Reading and writing (WORKBOOK pp.43–44)

4. WB p.43 **Activity** ④ Puzzle. Have students solve the word jumbles and write out the sentences.

Answers
2. The doll comes from China. It's Chinese.
3. The book comes from England. It's English.
4. The statue comes from Greece. It's Greek.
5. The hat comes from Russia. It's Russian.
6. The plate comes from Spain. It's Spanish.

5. **Activity** ⑤ Ask: *What's wrong with these sentences?* Have students correct the sentences first orally, then in writing.

Answers
2. Two women bought three knives.
3. Three men read three stories.
4. Two sheep chased four children.

6. WB p.44 **Activity** ⑥ Have students answer questions about their own country. These can be done orally before students write.

7. **Activity** ⑦ Have students find twelve words in the word search square. These words are all on p.44 in the Student Book.

Answers

```
Q Z C A R S G K Z T R
W O O D X N Q H M X A
B E M K C K T D A J D
P A P E R H O N T C I
T N U S D Y K Z S L O
M O T O R C Y C L E S
L C E U Y H O B B Y C
F O R I G A M I X G Z
Y J S V C A P I T A L
T E L E V I S I O N S
```

Ending the lesson

8. (Extra) Drawing and writing: Have students draw aspects of Japan and write sentences about them. This can then be made into a wall display for the classroom.

UNIT 12

Lesson One

Language focus
Talking about cause and effect: *so ...*
Talking about the weather.

New words
sunglasses   turn on   turn off   record player   so

Review/Warm-up

1. Review *I'll*: Say: *I'm going shopping. I'll buy [a bag of marbles]. What will you buy [George]? (You'll buy [a bag of marbles] and I'll buy [a stamp album]).* Continue around the class, with each student adding an item to the list.

2. Review weather vocabulary (see *American Chatterbox* 2, Unit 6). Ask: *Is it raining today? Is it sunny? Are there clouds in the sky? Is it hot? Is it cold? Is it windy?*

Presentation (STUDENT BOOK p.45)

3. *So ...* Pre-teach *so.* Say: *I'm tired so I'll sit down.* Suit the actions to the words. Write on the board: *I'm tired so I'll sit down.* Then erase the words *tired* and *sit down.* Write in the place of *tired* the word *hungry.* Say: *I'm hungry so ...* Students supply the missing words, e.g., *eat a pizza.*

- Books open: Pre-teach new words: *sunglasses* by referring to the picture. Read the sentences aloud. Have students listen and repeat.
- Books closed. Say the first parts of the sentences in the books: *It's raining ...*, etc. Get students to complete the sentences: *... so I'll open my umbrella.*

Practice (STUDENT BOOK p.45, CS32)

4. Before listening: Pre-teach *record player.* Say: *I want to play my new record so I need a record player.* Pre-teach *turn on* and *turn off.* Tell students that they are going to hear a story about Jane and her father. Ask questions about the pictures: *Look at the first picture. What's Jane's dad doing? (He's reading his newspaper.) Is he happy? (No, he isn't.) What's Jane doing? (She's listening to music.),* etc.

- Play CS32. Have students listen to the story.
- Play CS32. Have students listen and point.

Tapescript

Voice 1: Listen and point.
Voice 2: Jane's dad wasn't very happy. He wanted to read his newspaper quietly, but Jane turned on her record player.
(Students point to picture 1)
Her music was very loud so her dad closed the door of the living room.
(Students point to picture 2)
But the music was still too loud so Jane's dad closed the window of the living room. But the music was still too loud.
(Students point to picture 3)
Suddenly, Jane's dad had an idea!
(Students point to picture 4)
He opened the door and the window and he turned on the television. It was very loud!
(Students point to picture 5)
Jane turned off her record player and came into the living room. She shouted angrily, "Dad, that television program is too loud. I can't hear my pop music so I'm going to my friend's house."
(Students point to picture 6)
Jane's dad smiled slowly and said, "Bye then," so Jane ran out of the house angrily.
(Students point to picture 7)
Then Jane's dad quickly turned off the television and started to read his newspaper. "That's better!" he laughed.
(Students point to picture 8)

- Play CS32 again. Have students listen and repeat.

5. Write these scrambled sentences on the board:
   a. her dad/Jane's music/so/the door/was/closed/very loud/of the living room. (Jane's music was very loud so her dad closed the door of the living room).
   b. so/my friend's/I/my pop music/can't/I'm/house/hear/going to (I can't hear my pop music so I'm going to my friend's house).
   c. angrily/out of/dad/so/Jane's/Jane/the house/"Bye then"/said/ran (Jane's dad said, "Bye then," so Jane ran out of the house angrily).

- Pair work: Have students write out the correct sentences.

6. Tell the story again: Ask questions about the story. As you ask, build up a story, getting students to write key sentences on the board. Ask: *Where was Jane's dad? (in the living room) What did he want to do? (He wanted to read his newspaper.) What did Jane turn on?*

UNIT 12

(She turned on her record player.) What was the music like? (It was very loud.) So what did her dad do? (He closed the door of the living room.) Was the music still too loud? (Yes, it was.) So what did Jane's dad do then? (He closed the door.) Who had an idea? (Jane's dad). What did he do? (He opened the door and the window and turned on the television.) Was the television very loud? (Yes, it was.) So what did Jane do? (She turned off her record player and came into the living room). Was she angry? (Yes, she was.) Did she shout? (Yes, she did.) Where did she want to go? (to her friend's house). Why did she want to go there? (because the television was too loud). What did Jane's dad say? ("Bye then.") What did Jane do? (She ran out of the house.) Did Jane's dad turn off the television? (Yes, he did.) What did he start to do? (He started to read his newspaper.)

Reading and writing (WORKBOOK p.45)

7.   Activity ① Read and match. Do the first example with the whole class.

Answers   1. e   2. h   3. b   4. a   5. g   6. d   7. c   8. f

8.   Activity ② Magic sentence tricks. Demonstrate on the board how the "trick" works. Use the short sentences on SB p.45 as extra examples. Do the Workbook examples orally first.

Answers
1. It's made of metal, so you can't bend it.
2. She comes from Canada, so she speaks French and English.
3. There isn't any gravity, so astronauts float around in space.
4. Crocodiles have sharp teeth, so they are dangerous.
5. Movie directors today can use many special effects, so they make more exciting movies.

Ending the lesson

9. Writing: Have students, in pairs, complete the sentences. Explain that these should be in the past tense, like the story on CS32.
1. I was hungry so ...
2. I was thirsty so ...
3. I was sleepy so ...
4. I was cold so ...
5. I wanted to give my friend a present so ...

Lesson Two

Language focus
Review: *somebody, anybody, nobody, everybody*

New words
clap (verb)   *hid* (past tense)   *seat*   *afraid*

Review/Warm-up

1. Review *so*. Ask students to complete the sentences: *It's raining so ...; It's cold so ...; It's hot so ...; It's windy so ...*

2. Review Egyptian vocabulary from *American Chatterbox 3*, Unit 13: *pyramid, stone, pharaoh, king, queen.*

Story presentation (STUDENT BOOK p.46, CS33)

3. *The Queen's Magician.* The story so far: When Uncle John met Kashoki, the Japanese magician, Kashoki told him that the missing pages from the Book of Adabra were in ancient Egypt. Unknown to Uncle John and the children, Spider Smith was listening. He too wants to find the missing pages.
- Before listening: Ask questions about the story so far: *Where are the missing pages? (in Egypt, in a pyramid). Where are Uncle John and the children going to go next? (to Egypt). Does Spider Smith know about the missing pages? (Yes, he does.)*
- Prediction: Ask students to predict what will happen next: *How will Uncle John and the children go to Egypt? What will they see there? What will they find there? What will Spider Smith do?*
- Pre-teach *seat*. Say: *You sit on a seat in the bus.*
- Write focus questions on the board:
    a. What did Spider Smith do?   (He followed them and hid the Time Machine.)
    b. What was the date in Egypt?   (2500 BC)
    c. What was the pyramid like?   (It was made of stone and was very big.)
    d. Who came out of the pyramid?   (the Queen's Magician)
    e. What did the magician say?   ("I'm going to get into the basket with the snakes.")
- Books open. Play CS33. Have students listen and read.
- Play CS33 again. Have students listen and answer the focus questions.
- Ask students to guess the meanings of *afraid* and *hid* from the context, and *clap* from picture four.

Story practice

4. Ask further questions about the story: *Where did Spider Smith hide in the Time Machine? (behind a seat). What did the children see when they went outside the Time Machine? (the Nile River and a pyramid). Who was the beautiful woman? (Queen Neops). What did the Queen's Magician do? (some magic tricks). What was the magician's next trick like? (very dangerous). Who climbed into the basket? (the magician). Did he come out of the basket? (no). Who looked inside the basket? (a woman). Did she see the magician? (no).*

5. Dialogue: Write the following lines on the board and ask students to say who said them:
That's Queen Neops. She's looking at her new pyramid. (a man)
Look! Is that the Book of Adabra? (Caroline)
I'm going to get into the basket with the snakes. (the Queen's magician)
Look inside the basket. (the Queen)
The magician isn't here! (a woman)

6. Writing: Pair work: Ask students to complete this letter from Spider Smith to Ringo Dingo.

> Dear Ringo,
> I hid inside the ... ... and followed John Jones to ...
> Nobody ... me.
> There was a very big ... It was made of ... A ... came out of the pyramid. Then he did some ...
> ... Everybody ... and ...
> Then I saw the ... of ...!
> I have a plan. I will get the ... of ... and the missing ...!
> Your friend,
>
> Spider.

Presentation (STUDENT BOOK p.47, CS34)

7. *Somebody, anybody, everybody.* Books open: Point to the pictures and ask: *Where are these people? (inside a pyramid) Is it frightening? How many people are there in the first picture/in the second picture/in the third picture/in the fourth picture/in the last picture? Is somebody leaving in the second picture?* Have students answer.
- Play CS34. Have students listen.
- Explain that *What's nobody doing?* is a nonsense question, therefore hardly ever used in real life.
- Play CS34 again. Have students listen and repeat.

Tapescript

Voice 1: Listen and repeat.
Voice 2: Is there anybody there?
Yes, everybody's there ...
No, somebody is leaving ...
Somebody else is leaving ...
Somebody else is leaving ...
Now there's nobody there.
What's nobody doing?
Nothing!

Practice (STUDENT BOOK p.47)

8. Ask questions about the classroom: *Is there anybody in the corner? (Yes, there is/No, there isn't.) Who's in the closet? (Nobody). Is [George] near the window? Is anybody else near the window?*, etc.

Reading and writing (WORKBOOK p.46)

9. **Activity** ③ Have students read the story in their Student Book again and then rearrange the sentences to make a summary. Have students read the sentences out loud in sequence.

Answers Spider Smith hid behind the seats inside the Time Machine, and so he went from Australia to Egypt with Uncle John and the children. When they arrived in Egypt, they saw the Nile River and an enormous new pyramid, made of stone. Queen Neops and her magician were at the new pyramid. The magician wanted to show the Queen some new magic tricks. The magician had the Book of Adabra in his hand. He did a dangerous trick from the Book with some poisonous snakes in a basket. The magician climbed into the basket ... and he disappeared. The Queen was afraid.

10. Activity ④ Puzzle: Have students write out the message from Queen Neops.

Answers Please come to my ghost party. Bring all your friends. We'll have black cat cookies and famous Pharaoh food to eat. Come to the Pyramid of the Dead at one o'clock, when Venus is in the sky.

Ending the lesson

11. Survey: Group work: Have students ask and answer about likes and dislikes: *Do you like chocolate? (Yes, I do./No, I don't.)* Then ask them to make sentences about their group: *Everybody in our group likes ... Nobody in our group likes ... Somebody in our group likes ...*

UNIT 12

12. Pair work: Combine sentences with *so*. Write the following sentences on one side of the board:

1. Spider Smith wanted to go to Egypt.
2. Kate wanted to know about the beautiful woman.
3. The people enjoyed the magic tricks.
4. The Queen was afraid.

On the other side of the board write:
... they laughed and clapped.
... she told a woman to look inside the basket.
... she asked a man about her.
... he hid inside the Time Machine.

Working in pairs, students combine the sentences with *so*, then write them down.

Answers
1. Spider Smith wanted to go to Egypt so he hid inside the Time Machine.
2. Kate wanted to know about the beautiful woman so she asked a man about her.
3. The people enjoyed the magic tricks so they laughed and clapped.
4. The Queen was afraid so she told a woman to look inside the basket.

Lesson Three

Language focus
Review: Past simple.

New words
cotton   dancing   gold   meat   wife   wives

Review/Warm-up

1. Review vocabulary: Write the following word jumbles on the board: TASE (seat), DIMRAPY (pyramid), TESKBA (basket), SANKE (snake), ENQUE (queen), LINE VIRRE (Nile River); NOTES (stone).

Reading (STUDENT BOOK p.48)

2. *Ancient Egypt*. Before reading: Pre-teach *meat* and *wife/wives* by translation.
- Books open. Say: *Point to the Nile River. Point to the pharaoh. Point to the queen. Point to the musicians. Point to a pyramid. Point to the jewelry.* Students point.
- Pre-teach *gold* by referring to the pictures.
- Write focus questions on the board:
  a. When did the ancient Egyptians live? (about 5,000 years ago)
  b. What did the Egyptians catch in the Nile River? (fish)
  c. How many wives did a pharaoh often have? (three or four)
  d. What were the Egyptians' clothes made of? (cotton or wool)
- Reading: Have students read passage silently. Go around the class helping them. Have students answer the focus questions.
- After reading: Ask further questions about the passage: *Did anybody live inside the pyramids? (No, they were houses for dead pharaohs.) Where were the pictures of the pharaohs? (inside the pyramid). What can we learn about from these pictures? (the lives of the pharaohs). Who often had music and dancing? (the pharaohs).*
- Ask students to guess the meanings of *cotton* and *dancing* from the context.

3. Pair work: Have students work out the answers to the focus questions in the book in pairs.

Answers
1. Because they needed water from the Nile for their farms, and because they caught fish from the river.
2. The king of ancient Egypt was called the Pharaoh.
3. There was food, clothes, beds, tables, and chairs for the dead king.
4. They were made of gold and colorful stones.
5. They ate cheese, meat, grapes, peas, bread, milk, and fish.

Reading and writing (WORKBOOK pp.47–48)

4. WB p.47 Activity ⑤ Have students choose words from the box to complete the description.

Answers   thousand, built, pyramids, put, food, gold, inside, stole, front, so, rocks, treasure, museum, city

5. Activity ⑥ Have students complete the words.

Answers   1. jewelry   2. vase   3. mask   4. statue
5. knife

6. WB p.48 **Activity ⑦** Tell students to look at SB p.48 again to find the words to complete this puzzle.

Answers

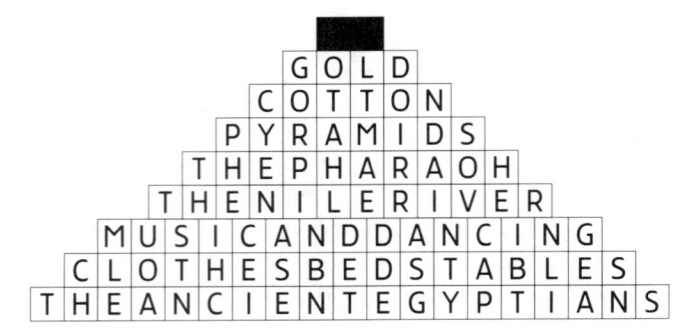

```
            G O L D
          C O T T O N
        P Y R A M I D S
      T H E P H A R A O H
    T H E N I L E R I V E R
  M U S I C A N D D A N C I N G
C L O T H E S B E D S T A B L E S
T H E A N C I E N T E G Y P T I A N S
```

Ending the lesson

7. (Extra) Project: Have students make a wall display in the form of a labeled picture of ancient Egypt, showing the Nile River, a pyramid, musicians, etc.

UNIT 13

Lesson One

Language focus
Review: Past simple.
Talking about travel: *by plane/boat/train.*

New words
by (+ transport)   *France*   *French*   *drank* (past tense)

Review/Warm-up

1. Review past simple: Ask questions about the story: *Where did Uncle John and the children go in the Time Machine? What did they see there? What was the weather like on Mars? (cold) What was the weather like in Australia? (hot and dry),* etc.

Presentation (STUDENT BOOK p.49, CS35)

2. *Lucky's trip to Europe.* Books closed. Pre-teach *by train*, etc. Say: *I came here by bus today.* Write the sentence on the board. Ask: *Did you come here by bus, [Maria]? How did you come here?* Review kinds of transportation known to students. Ask them to make sentences: *Spider went to Japan by plane. Uncle John went to Mars by Time Machine,* etc.
- Books open. Point to the map: Say: *This is a map of Europe.* Ask: *Which countries can you see on the map?* Use the map to pre-teach *France* and *French.*

3. Listen and point to the countries.
- Play CS35. Have students listen.
- Play CS35 again. Have students listen and point to the countries on the map.

4. Listen and match the pictures. Play CS35 again. Have students listen and point to the pictures.

Tapescript

Answers
Voice 1: Listen and point to the right countries.
Voice 2: First, Lucky went by plane to England. It rained in England. She saw Tower Bridge in London. And she drank some English tea.
(Students point to A)
Then Lucky went by boat to France. It snowed in France. She saw the Eiffel Tower in Paris – it was very high! And she had some French cheese.
(Students point to D)
Then Lucky went to Spain by car. It was very hot and sunny in Spain. Lucky saw a beautiful Spanish beach. She ate some Spanish oranges.

UNIT 13

(Students point to B)
Next, Lucky went by bus to Italy. It was sunny and hot in Italy too. Lucky saw the Leaning Tower in Pisa – it's a very strange building. She ate some Italian pizza.
(Students point to E)
Then Lucky went by train to Greece. It was very windy in Greece. Lucky saw the Parthenon in Athens – it's a very old and beautiful building. And she ate some Greek yogurt.
(Students point to C)

5. Pair work: Have students copy and complete the chart.

country	went by	weather	saw	ate
England				
		very windy		
	bus			
				cheese
			beach	

Practice (STUDENT BOOK p.49)

6. Ask and answer: Have students ask and answer the questions in the book about all the countries that Lucky visited.

- Pair work: Have students practice this interview with Lucky:

Interviewer: How did you travel to England?
Lucky Lorenz: By *(plane)*.
Interviewer: What was the weather like?
Lucky Lorenz: *(It rained)*.
Interviewer: What did you see there?
Lucky Lorenz: I saw *(Tower Bridge in London)*.
Interviewer: What did you eat or drink?
Lucky Lorenz: *(I drank some English tea)*.

Have students practice the interview several times, substituting the words in brackets with details of the other countries that Lucky visited.

Answers
1. She traveled to England by plane.
2. No, it wasn't. It rained in England.
3. She saw Tower Bridge.
4. She drank some English tea.

Reading and writing (WORKBOOK p.49)

7. Activity ① Have students match the people, the countries and the transportation. Then have them write sentences.

Answers
2. Mr. Wizzo went to Kenya by plane.
3. Kashoki went to China by train.
4. Spider Smith went to Australia by boat.
5. Miss Electra went to Brazil by plane.
6. Ringo Dingo went to Japan by boat.

Ending the lesson

8. (Extra) Drawing and writing: Have students draw and write postcards from Lucky to her friends. For example:

```
I am in _____
now. I came
here by _____.     Mr. Wizzo
I ate _____
here and I          Los Angeles, CA
saw _____.         unum
          Lucky.
```

Lesson Two

Language focus
Review: Verbs.

New words
away fast verb

Review/Warm-up

1. Review *by train*, etc. Ask questions: *Can you go to Mars by bus? Can you go to Egypt by bicycle? Would you like to go to China by boat?*, etc.

Story presentation (STUDENT BOOK p.50, CS36)

2. *Spider steals the Book!* The story so far: Uncle John and the children are in ancient Egypt, in search of the missing pages from the Book of Adabra. They do not know, but Spider Smith hid in the Time machine and traveled to Egypt with them. Queen Neops's magician climbed into a basket of snakes and then disappeared.

- Before reading: Ask questions about the story so far: *Where are Uncle John and the children? (in Egypt) Who did some magic tricks? (the Queen's Magician) What did the magician climb into? (a basket) Who looked inside the basket? (a woman) Did she see the magician? (no).*
- Pre-teach *fast*. Say: *A train is fast, but a plane is faster.* Ask: *Is a car faster than a bicycle?*
- Prediction: Ask: *Will they see the Queen's Magician again? Will Spider Smith steal the Book of Adabra?*

- Write focus questions on the board:
  a. Where was the magician? (on top of the pyramid)
  b. Who saw Spider Smith? (Caroline)
  c. Who had the Book of Adabra? (Spider Smith)
  d. What happened to Spider? (He fell into the river.)
  e. Who took the pages out of the Book of Adabra? (Queen Neops)
  f. Where did they put the pages? (inside the pyramid)
- Books open. Play CS36. Have students listen and read.
- Play CS36 again. Have students listen and answer the focus questions.
- Ask students to try to guess the meaning of *away* from the context.

Story practice

3. Ask further questions about the story: *Why did Spider look inside the basket? (Because he wanted the Book of Adabra.) Did he find the Book? (yes). What did the snakes do? (They came out of the basket.) Who pulled the Queen away from the snakes? (Uncle John). Where did Spider run? (to the river). Who ran after him? (the children and Barker). Who ran faster, the children or Spider? (the children). What did Barker do? (He attacked Spider.) What did Kate do? (She pulled the Book away from Spider.) Who took the Book from Kate? (the Queen). Which trick was too dangerous? (the trick with the snakes). So what did the Queen do? (She took seven pages from the Book of Adabra and put them in a box.) Who put the box inside the pyramid? (a soldier). What are Uncle John and the children going to do? (go back to the pyramid later).*

4. Dialogue: Write the following lines on the board and ask students to say who said them.
"Look out, Queen Neops!" (Uncle John)
"Look! There's Spider! What's he doing here?" (Caroline)
"Help!" (Spider)
"Thank you." (Queen Neops)
"He has the Book!" (Caroline)
"Come on, Barker! Quick!" (Kate)
"Queen Neops, look up there!" (a man)

5. Summary: Ask students to complete this extract from Kate's diary:
Suddenly we saw ... on top of the ... Then ... saw ... He found ... inside the ..., but the ... came out ... ran to the river and we chased him. Barker ... Spider, and Spider ... The Queen took ... from me and said, "..." The trick with the snakes was too ..., so the Queen took ... pages from ... and put them into a ... Then a soldier took ... and put it inside the ...

Presentation (STUDENT BOOK p.51, CS37)

6. *Verb games.* Books open: Ask questions about the pictures: *What's the girl doing? (She's whispering.),* etc.
- Play CS37. Have students listen and point to the right verbs.

Answers Jane/America/by boat
Joanna/Canada/by plane
John/Russia/by train

Tapescript

Voice 1: Listen and point.
  One. (Students point to *whisper*)
  Two. (Students point to *clap*)
  Three. (Students point to *laugh*)
  Four. (Students point to *shout*)
  Five. (Students point to *dance*)
  Six. (Students point to *climb*)
  Seven. (Students point to *walk*)
  Eight. (Students point to *run*)
  Nine. (Students point to *bark*)
  Ten. (Students point to *cry*)
  Eleven. (Students point to *crunch*)
  Twelve. (Students point to *roar*)

Practice (STUDENT BOOK p.51)

7. *Bingo.* Have each student choose four verbs and cover them with counters or pieces of paper. Call out the twelve verbs in random order. The first student to shout "Bingo" and have all four words correct is the winner.
- Play the game several times, always calling out the verbs in a different order.

Reading and writing (WORKBOOK p.50)

8. Activity ② Have students read the story in their Student Books again and answer the questions.

Answers 1. on top of the pyramid
2. the snakes
3. Uncle John
4. Kate
5. a soldier

9. Activity ③ Have students read and fill in the boxes. Check the answers, then ask and answer: *Where did Jane come from? How did she come?,* etc.

UNIT 13

Ending the lesson

10. (Extra) Dictation: Dictate the following passage. *The magician did a very good trick./The trick was too dangerous/so the Queen took seven pages/from the Book./She put the pages into a box/ and gave the box to a soldier.*
    - Follow the usual dictation procedure. Then ask one student to come to the board, without his/her book. Ask another student to dictate the first five words. The student at the board writes what he/she hears. The rest of the class must remain silent during this phase. Then another two students take over and dictate and write the next five words, and so on until the whole dictation is on the board. Finally, the whole class helps correct the dictation. Ask another student to go to the board to make any corrections the other students ask for.

Lesson Three

Language focus
Review: Past simple

New words
European   invented (past tense)   half   alphabet   letter
Roman   writing

Review/Warm-up

1. Review verbs from SB p. 51. Play CS37 again. Students say: *She's whispering,* etc., after each sound effect.

2. Review: *China/Chinese,* etc. Write on the board: *Britain, Spain, France, Greece, Italy, Egypt, China, Japan.* Have students come to the board and write next to these *British, Spanish,* etc. Refer students to the map on SB p.49, and explain that all those countries are *European.*

Reading (STUDENT BOOK p.52)

3. *Ancient writing.* Before reading: Pre-teach new words: *invented, half, alphabet, letter,* and *Roman* by translation.
   - Write focus questions on the board:
     a. Where did the ancient Romans live? (in Italy)
     b. Which alphabet do people in Greece use? (the Greek alphabet)
     c. How old is the Chinese alphabet? (4,000 years old)
     d. Which alphabet used pictures for words? (the Egyptian alphabet)
   - Scanning: Books open: Have students find the new words in the passage.
   - Reading: Have students read the passage. Go around the class helping them. Have students answer the focus questions.
   - Some students may be interested to know more about the various writing systems, so the following notes may be useful:
     1. There are twenty-six letters in the Roman alphabet, and twenty-four in the Greek alphabet. However, not all European languages which use the Roman system have all twenty-six letters. The ancient Romans themselves wanted only twenty-one letters: j, y and v, w and g were used as alternative forms of i, u, and c respectively, and these alternative forms gradually developed as separate letters with separate sounds.
     2. The Chinese characters are not an alphabet as such, but ideograms: pictorial representations which also represent words of similar sounds.
     3. Hieroglyphics, the ancient Egyptian system of writing, developed in a similar way to Chinese writing, with pictures representing words.

4. Pair work: Have students find the answers to the questions on SB p.52.

   Answers
   1. English uses the Roman alphabet.
   2. There are twenty-four letters in the Greek alphabet.
   3. No, it isn't.
   4. There are 47,000 characters In Chinese today.
   5. The ancient Egyptian alphabet is the oldest.

5. Complete the information sheet: Pair work: Write this outline on the board. Have students complete it with information from the passage.

   Ancient writing
   The oldest alphabet.
   An alphabet with twenty-six letters:
   An alphabet with twenty-four letters:
   An alphabet with 47,000 characters:
   An alphabet with pictures for words:

Reading and writing (WORKBOOK pp.51–52)

6. WB p.51 **Activity** ④ Have students put the verbs into the past tense and complete the sentences.

Answers had, put on, took, listened, watched, did, laughed, clapped, liked, ate

7. **Activity** ⑤ Magic numbers. Have students work out the puzzle. Some students may have difficulty understanding the code. Each letter is represented by one of the numbers from one to nine. So, after each group of nine letters, the numbers start from number one again. To get the final magic number, all the numbers representing the letters of the person's name are added together, e.g., K=2, E=5, N=5 reaching a total of 12. The two digits are then added together (1 + 2) to make the magic number 3. Students then work out their own magic numbers.

Answers Caroline's magic number is 5.

8. WB p.52 **Activity** ⑥ Have students find in the box the words missing from Spider Smith's letter and write the letter again.

Answers After, with, When, suddenly, inside, Then, quickly, and, and, into

Ending the lesson

9. (Extra) Have students invent their own picture alphabet for sending messages. In groups, they should invent pictures for this message: *The seven pages are in a box. The box is in the pyramid.* Then ask them to think of other messages. They should then pass these to other groups to decipher.

UNIT 14

Lesson One

Language focus
Review: Directions: *turn right/left, go straight.*

New words
crossroads   necklace   on the left   some more

Review/Warm-up

1. Review directions: Play the "Please and Thank you" game. Use these expressions: *turn left, turn right, go forward, go backward, stop.*

Presentation (STUDENT BOOK p.53, CS38)

2. *The Treasure in the pyramid.* Pre-teach *crossroads.* Draw a simple map on the board. Say: *This is the crossroads.* Get students to come to the board. Say: *Turn left at the crossroads. Go straight. Go over the crossroads.* Have students trace the route on the board.
- Pre-teach *some more.* Say: *There are some [books on my desk]. There are some more [books] in the room.* Ask: *Where are there some more [books]? (in the bookcase).* Continue to ask other, similar questions about the classroom.
- Books open. Say: *Point to the cat. Point to the mask. Point to the knives. Point to the boxes. Point to the bottles.* Pre-teach *necklace* by referring to the picture.

3. Listen and find the way to the treasure. Explain the expression *find the way to.*
- Play CS38. Students listen and trace the way through the maze. Stop the tape after each room is reached.
- Play CS38 again. Students listen and point to the treasure in each room. Stop the tape after each one and ask questions about the treasure: *What did you find in the blue room? (five knives) What are they made of? (metal) What did you find in the yellow room? (two bottles) What are the bottles made of? (stone) What did you find in the red room? (a statue of a cat) What's the statue of the cat made of? (black stone) What did you find in the brown room? (a necklace) What's the necklace made of? (gold) What did you find in the purple room? (three boxes) What are the boxes made of? (metal and colorful stones) What did you find in the green room? (the mask of the Pharaoh) What's the mask made of? (gold)*

UNIT 14

Tapescript

Answers

Voice 1: Listen and find the way to the six rooms of treasure.
Voice 2: Start at the south door.
Go straight, over the first crossroads to the second crossroads, then stop. Turn left and go straight. Then turn right. Turn right again into the blue room. You will find some treasure inside the blue room: five knives made of metal.
(Picture B)
Go out of the blue room and turn right. Then turn left into the yellow room. Inside the yellow room you will find some more treasure: two bottles made of stone.
(Picture F)
Go out of the yellow room and turn left. Go straight, over the crossroads. Turn right and then turn left and go into the red room. Inside the red room you will find some more treasure: a statue of a cat made of black stone.
(Picture E)
Go out of the red room and turn left. Go straight, over the crossroads. You can't go into the room on the left because it's closed. Go straight and turn right. Then turn right again and go into the brown room. You will find this treasure in the brown room: a gold necklace.
(Picture C)
Go out of the brown room and turn right. Go straight to the crossroads, then at the crossroads turn right again. Go straight to the next crossroads. Turn left. Then go straight and turn left again into the purple room. Inside the purple room you will find this treasure: three boxes made of metal and colorful stones.
(Picture A)
Go out of the purple room and turn right. Then go straight to the first crossroads. Turn left and go into the green room. Inside the green room you will find this treasure: the gold mask of the Pharaoh.
(Picture D)

Practice (STUDENT BOOK p.53)

4. Find your way to the treasure: Pair work: Practice finding the first room with the class. Give the instructions: *Start at the south door. Go straight, over the first crossroads to the second crossroads, then STOP. Turn left and go straight. Then turn right. Turn right again.* Ask: *Where are you? (in the blue room).*

- Have students, in pairs, give each other instructions for getting to the other rooms. Go around the class helping them.

Reading and writing (WORKBOOK p.53)

5. Activity ① Have students read and find the treasures on the island. Make sure that students go from the *Start here* square each time. This exercise can be done as pair work.

Answers 2. a silver spear. 3. an ancient Japanese mask. 4. some poisonous spiders. 5. an ancient Chinese vase. 6. a book of magic spells.

Ending the lesson

6. Writing: Ask students to complete these instructions: *How to go from the blue to the yellow room. Go out of the blue room and turn ... Then turn ... into the ... room. Inside the ... room you will ... some more ... ... made of ...*

7. (Extra) Finding your way: Arrange the furniture in the classroom to make a street grid, or go outside. Have students work in pairs, one as a driver, and the other as a passenger. They "drive" side by side. The passenger gives the driver instructions to get to a certain place.

Be prepared!

Bring drawing materials for Lesson Two.

Lesson Two

Language focus
Talking about fears: *afraid of ...*

New words
at first   at last   candle   frightened   toward

Review/Warm-up

1. Review directions: Use the maze on SB p.53. Ask: *Where can I find the gold necklace? (in the brown room) How can I get from the red room to the brown room?* Have students explain.

Story presentation (STUDENT BOOK p.54, CS39)

2. *Inside the pyramid.* The story so far: Uncle John and the children are in Egypt. Spider Smith is there too. Spider Smith tried to steal the Book of Adabra, but Barker and the children rescued the Book, and Spider fell into the Nile River. Then they saw Queen Neops remove seven pages from the Book and put them in a box. She told a soldier to put the box in the pyramid.

- Before listening: Ask questions about the story so far: *Where are the missing pages? (in the pyramid). Who put them there? (a soldier). What happened to Spider Smith? (He fell into the river.)*

- Prediction: Ask: *Where will Uncle John and the children go next? What will they do there? What will Spider Smith do? Will it be dangerous?*
  Books closed. Pre-teach *at last*. Say: *Uncle John and the children went to America to look for the missing pages. Next they went to Australia. They didn't find the missing pages. Then they went to Japan, but the missing pages weren't there. Now they are in Egypt. At last they know the hiding place of the missing pages!*
- Write focus questions on the board:
  a. What did they see in the big room? (boxes, statues, and gold coins)
  b. What did Caroline see? (the box with the missing pages)
  c. What did they fall into? (a big hole)
  d. Why were the children frightened? (Because there were hundreds of snakes in the hole.)
  e. What did the snakes do? (They came nearer and nearer.)
- Books open. Pre-teach *candle*. Say: *Look at picture 1.* Ask: *What does Uncle John have? He has a candle.*
- Play CS39. Have students listen and read.
- Play CS39 again. Have students listen and answer the focus questions.
- After reading: Ask students to guess the meaning of *at first, toward,* and *frightened* from the context.

Story practice

3. Ask further questions about the story: *Was it dark inside the pyramid? (Yes, it was very dark.) How did they move? (on their hands and knees). Did they go quickly? (No, they went slowly.) Which way did they turn first? (left) Did they see Spider Smith? (no). Where was he? (behind some boxes). What happened when they ran toward the box? (They fell into a big hole.) Could they see anything at first? (no). Why not? (Because Caroline dropped the candle and it was dark.) What color were the snakes' eyes? (green). What did Spider do? (He went away.)*

4. Dialogue: Write the following pieces of dialogue on the board. Have students identify the speakers, then say how each speech was said.
Don't move! (Uncle John)
Look over there! I can see the box with the missing pages! (Caroline)
What is Spider going to do, Uncle John? (Kate)
Please, Spider, Help us! (Ken)

5. Summary: Write this extract from Kate's diary on the board. Have students fill in the blanks.
We went inside the ... Uncle John had Kashoki's ...and a ... We moved on our ... and ... We ... slowly. At ... we came to ... Suddenly, Caroline saw the ... so we ran ... the box. But we ... into a big ... Caroline ... the candle. At first, we could not see anything, but then I saw some ... ... There were ... in the hole! We were very ... Then we ... Spider Smith's face ... us. He looked ... at us and ... Then he went ... We waited and ... The snakes ... ...

Presentation (STUDENT BOOK p.55, CS40)

6. *What are you afraid of?* Pre-teach *afraid of*. Ask: *Were the children frightened in the pyramid? (yes) Why? (Because there were hundreds of snakes.)* Shudder artistically and say: *The children were afraid of the snakes.* Ask: *Are you afraid of snakes?*
- Books open. Read the questions and answers out loud.
- Play CS40. Have students listen.
- Play CS40 again. Have students listen and repeat.

Tapescript

Voice 1: Listen and repeat.
Ken: Are you afraid of spiders?
Kate: No, I'm not.
Kate: Are you afraid of the dark?
Ken: Yes, I am.

- Say: *Look at the pictures. Point to the snakes. Point to the monsters.* Students point. Ask: *Are you afraid of ghosts, [George]?*, etc.

Practice (STUDENT BOOK p.55)

7. Pair work: Have students ask and answer questions about the pictures. Go around the class listening and helping where necessary.

Reading and writing (WORKBOOK p.54)

8. Activity ② Have students read the story in their Student Book again and make sentences.

Answers
1. Uncle John and the children went inside the pyramid.
2. They saw some boxes of gold coins in a big room.
3. Suddenly they fell into a big hole with hundreds of snakes in it.
4. Spider Smith looked down at them in the hole and laughed.
5. The children and Uncle John waited and listened.

9. Activity ③ Have students write sentences, using the chart as a guide. Do an example orally before students write.

UNIT 14

Answers
2. Caroline is afraid of spiders, ghosts, and big dogs. She isn't afraid of snakes
3. Kate is afraid of the dark, angry teachers, and snakes. She isn't afraid of insects.
4. Uncle John is afraid of water. He isn't afraid of ghosts.

Then have students complete the chart for themselves and write sentences.

Ending the lesson

10. (Extra) Drawing competition: Have students draw monsters, competing to draw the most frightening monster. As an extension, ask students to write about their monsters: *My monster looks like a dinosaur with very sharp teeth. It is green,* etc. Ask questions about the monsters: *Is [George's] monster more frightening than [Maria's]? Whose monster is the most frightening?*

Be prepared!

Bring drawing materials for Lesson Three.

Lesson Three

Language focus
Review: Past simple.

New words
answer (noun)   rest (=remainder)

Review/Warm-up

1. Review *afraid of*. Ask questions: *Are you afraid of the dark? Were the children afraid of the snakes? Is Uncle John afraid of Spider Smith? Are you afraid of crocodiles?*, etc.

2. Review past simple: Write a list of verbs on the board: *do, see, say, go, arrive, make, use, help*. Have students come to the board and write the past simple form.

Reading (STUDENT BOOK p.56)

3. *Make a story*. Before reading: Books closed. Pre-teach *answer*. Write on the board: *Where did you go? I went to the swimming pool.* Say: *Point to the question. Read the question.* Have students read the question out loud. Then say: *Now point to the answer. Read the answer, please.* Have students read the answer.

- Write focus questions on the board:
  a. What was the Time Machine made of? (boxes, pieces of metal)
  b. Who helped make the Time Machine? (friends)
- Books open. Have students read the handwritten passage and answer the focus questions.
- Explain that students are going to write their own story. They should start by copying the handwritten section. They should include some more materials for building the Time Machine, and their friends' own names in the story.
- Pre-teach *rest of*. Say: *The book started the story. You are going to write the rest of the story.*
- Do a version of the continuation of the story orally with the whole class. Ask different students to choose answers for the questions.

4. Students write, choosing answers as they go along to make their own story. Go around the class, helping them.
- Pair work: Have students read and check each other's stories, in pairs.
- Ask questions about the stories: *Where did you go in the Time Machine, [George]? When did you arrive there, [Maria]?*, etc.
- Select two or three students to read their stories aloud.

Reading and writing (WORKBOOK pp.55–56)

5. WB p.55 **Activity ④** Have students use the words to write a story. This activity can be done with the whole class, writing the story on the board as students suggest words.

Answers
1. He saw a table and chairs in the middle of a small room. He saw gold plates, cups, and food on the table too.
2. Spider went into the room. Suddenly a ghost stood up and pointed angrily at Spider. Spider turned and ran.
3. He ran and ran. It was dark and he had no candle. Suddenly he came to a big room. It had/There was a black hole in the middle.
4. Spider Smith went toward the hole. He looked down into the hole. He started to laugh.

6. Activity ⑤ Spelling: Have students fill in the missing letters.

Answers   photograph, telephone, alphabet, scissors, scientist

7. WB p.56 **Activity** ⑥ Have students circle the different word in each sentence. After checking the answers, ask students why the words were different.

Answers   2. climb   3. Italy   4. frightened   5. magician
6. happiest   7. actor   8. nurse   9. circle   10. factory
11. space

8. **Activity** ⑦ In this vocabulary exercise, students sort the words into categories: time, jobs, animals.

Answers   In the clock: day, week, minute, month, second, year. In the computer: secretary, nurse, astronaut, cowboy, driver, builder, dancer, homemaker. In the cage: crocodile, kangaroo, sheep, jaguar, shark, bee.

Ending the lesson

9. Interviews: Pair work: Have students interview each other about their stories.
   A. *Where did you go in the Time Machine?*
   B: *I went to Australia,* etc.

10. (Extra) Group work: Drawing and writing. Ask students to draw the same story as a comic strip.

UNIT 15

Lesson One

Language focus
Review: Comparatives/superlatives. Future simple, Irregular past tense

Review/Warm-up

1. Review: *afraid of.* Ask: *What are you afraid of? Are you afraid of the dark? Are you afraid of ghosts?,* etc.

2. Review past simple: Write the following answers on the board.
   I went to Japan.
   I arrived there in the past.
   I visited a city.
   I saw a magician.
   I said "Hello."
• Ask students to tell you the questions to go with the answers: *Where did you go? When did you arrive there? What did you do? What did you see? What did you say?*

Review (STUDENT BOOK p.57)

3. *Look again, please (Review).* Books open.
• **Adjectives:** Say: *Find the word "long."* Students point. Read out loud: *long, longer, longest.* Get students to write the comparative and superlative forms on the board: *cold, colder, the coldest,* etc.
• **Will:** Practice the sample question and answer: *Will Spider Smith find the Book of Adabra? Yes, he will./No, he won't.*
• Irregular past: Say: *Point to the word "run,"* etc. Students point.

Practice (STUDENT BOOK p.57)

4. Have students practice adjectives by referring back to Units 4 and 6.
• Turn to p.13 Ask and answer: *Which line is longer?,* etc.
• Turn to p.15 Ask and answer: *Which trick is more dangerous?,* etc.
• Turn to p.21 Ask and answer: *Which magician is the tallest?,* etc.
• Turn to p.23 Ask and answer: *Which sport is the most dangerous?,* etc.

5. Have students practice *will* by referring back to Unit 9.
• Turn to p.33. Play the game *Explore treasure island* again.
• Turn to p.35. Play CS22 again: Have students listen and answer.

UNIT 15

6. Have students practice the irregular past by referring to the story episodes. Group work: Have students complete to find as many as possible of the verbs on the list in the story, making a note of the Unit in which these appear. The group to find the most verbs wins.

- Game: "Past tense race." Books closed. Divide the class into two teams. Make the first students from each team stand in front of the board, each with a piece of chalk. Call out a verb from the list on SB p.57. The first student to write the correct irregular past tense scores a point for his/her team. Two more students come to the front and repeat the process.

Reading and writing (WORKBOOK p.57)

7. Activity 1 Have students choose the correct form of the adjective to complete the sentences.

Answers 2. shorter 3. prettiest 4. better
5. more interesting 6. most famous 7. best

8. Activity 2 Have students predict what will happen in the story. Ask the questions orally after the students have written short answers. This exercise asks students for opinions, so there are no right or wrong answers.

9. Activity 3 Have students find ten irregular past tense verbs in the square.

Answers

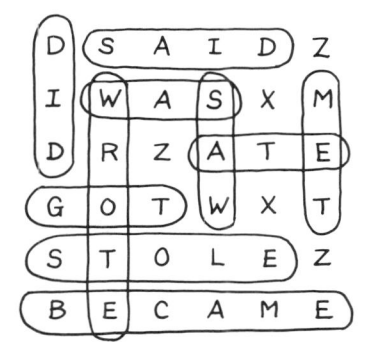

Ending the lesson

10. (Extra) Review superlatives by asking questions about the story. Write the following questions on the board:
1. Who was the best magician in the story?
2. What was the most frightening place of the story?
3. Who was the most dangerous person in the story?
4. What was the coldest place in the story?
5. Who was the meanest person in the story?

Lesson Two

Language focus
Greetings.

New words
garden Good evening light (= opposite of dark) really sunshine

---

Review/Warm-up

1. Review and practice irregular past tense verbs by asking questions: *Where did Spider Smith hide in the Time Machine? (He hid behind the seats.) Where did Spider Smith fly from Australia? (He flew to Japan.) What did Ringo Dingo steal from Kashoki? (He stole a box.) What did Spider Smith fall into? (He fell into the Nile River.) Who did Uncle John and the children meet in Hollywood? (They met Lucky Lorenz.)*, etc.

Story presentation (STUDENT BOOK p.58, CS41)

2. *Home again!* The story so far: Uncle John and the children are in a dangerous position. They are inside the pyramid. They found the box with the missing pages. But when they ran forward to get the box, they all fell into a big hole of snakes. Spider Smith saw them, but he laughed and went away. Now the snakes are getting nearer and nearer.

- Before listening: Ask questions about the story so far: *Where are they? (inside the pyramid) Is it dangerous? (yes) Why? (Because they are in a hole with hundreds of snakes.) What are the snakes doing? (They are coming nearer and nearer.)*
- Write focus questions on the board:
  a. Did they get out of the hole? (yes)
  b. Who helped them? (Spider Smith)
  c. Who took the missing pages out of the box? (Caroline)
  d. What did Barker do in the Time Machine? (ate some bones)
  e. Where did the Time Machine arrive? (in New York, in Kate's backyard)
- Play CS41. Have students listen and read.
- Play CS41 again. Have students listen and answer the focus questions.
- Get students to guess the meanings of *really* from the context.

Story practice

3. Ask further questions about the story: *What did Spider throw into the hole? (a ladder). What was the ladder made of? (rope). Who climbed out of the hole first? (Kate). What happened when Uncle John said a magic spell? (the Time Machine arrived). Why was everybody very happy in the Time Machine? (Because they had the Book of Adabra and the missing pages./Because they escaped from the pyramid.) What would Spider Smith like to be? (a good magician). Why was Kate's mother angry? (Because they were late for lunch.) What did Spider Smith give Kate's mom? (some beautiful flowers).*

4. Dialogue: Write the following on the board. Ask students to read the story and identify the speakers.
*What's that, John? (Kate's mom)
Of course I will. (Uncle John)
Catch this! (Spider Smith)
5, 6, 7 ... SHAZAM! (Uncle John)
Uh, Mom, this is Spider Smith. He'd like to be a magician. (Kate)*

5. Summary: Have students complete this letter from Spider Smith to Ringo Dingo.

> *Dear Ringo,*
>
> *I am not going to come back to Australia. I am going to stay in ... and learn to be a ... ... John Jones will ... me.*
> *John Jones and the children ... the missing pages inside the ... I helped them. Then everybody came back to ... by ... ...*
> *Yours,*
>
> *Spider.*

Presentation (STUDENT BOOK p.59, CS42)

6. *Good morning when it's morning.* Pre-teach *light.* Ask: *Is it dark at night? (yes) Is it dark in the morning? (no).* Say: *It's light in the morning.* Pre-teach *sunshine.* Ask: *Is it sunny today?: Do you like sunshine?* Write *light* and *sunshine* on the board.
- Scanning: Books open: Have students find the new words in the rhyme.
- Say: *Look at the pictures. Point to the morning. Point to the night. Point to the sunshine. Point to the evening.*
- Play CS42. Have students listen.
- Play CS42 again. Have students listen and repeat.

Tapescript

Voice 1: Listen and repeat.
Voice 2: Good morning when it's morning.
Good night when it is night
Good evening when it's dark out
Good day when it is light.
Good morning to the sunshine.
Good evening to the sky.
And when it's time to go away
Goodbye
Goodbye
Goodbye.

Practice (STUDENT BOOK p.58)

7. Ask questions about the rhyme: *What do we say in the morning? (Good morning) What do we say at night? (Good night) What do we say in the evening? (Good evening) What do we say when it's time to go away? (Goodbye).*

8. Have students repeat the rhyme again, without the tape.

Reading and writing (WORKBOOK p.58)

9. Activity ④ Have students read the story in their Student Book again and answer the questions.

Answers
1. Spider Smith
2. the missing pages
3. They talked about their adventures.
4. in Kate's backyard
5. Spider Smith

10. Activity ⑤ Have students, in groups, do this quiz as a competition. The group to write in the most words in a given time wins the game.

Suggested answers   A. apple, Australia/Africa
B. basketball, Brazil   C. café, cat   D. December, driver
E. eight, Earth   F. fire fighter, fish   G. green, Greek
H. history, hospital   I. Italy, ice cream   J. June, judo
L. living room, lawyer   M. Mercury, milk   N. nurse, nine
O. office, orange   P. parrot, pink   R. road, robot
S. sandwich, silver   T. teacher, tiger   V. volleyball, vet
Y. yellow, yogurt

Ending the lesson

11. Ask students to put the following events from the story in the order in which they happened:
*Ringo Dingo's dog chased them. (3)
They found the missing pages. (6)
Lucky Lorenz told them about Spider Smith. (2)*

UNIT 15 **65**

Uncle John and the children met Magixo. (1)
They had a party. (7)
They went to Egypt. (5)
They bought a present for Kashoki. (4)

Lesson Three

Language focus
Review: Past simple.

Review/Warm-up

1. Say the rhyme *Good morning when it's morning* again. Have students try to recite it with books closed.

Review (STUDENT BOOK p.60, CS43)

2. *Can you remember? (Review).* Pair work: Ask and answer the questions. Tell students to look back in the book to find the answers if necessary.
- Play CS43. Have students listen and check their answers.

Tapescript

Answers
Voice 1: Listen and check your answers.
One.
Voice 2: Magixo was made of metal and glass.
Two.
Barker brought back Uncle John's magic wand.
Three.
Caroline found the envelope.
Four.
Miss Electra was a teacher too.
Five.
Mr. Wizzo was 110 years old.
Six.
Spider found a shopping list.
Seven.
The children bought a paper bird for Kashoki. Inside the bird there were chocolates.
Eight.
He put the pages from the Book of Adabra in the pyramid.

- Ask and answer the questions again with the whole class.

3. Asking questions: Play CS43 again, with books closed. Stop the tape after each answer. Have students listen to answers, then say the questions that go with them.

4. Story Quiz: Group work: Each group makes up three new questions about the story. Then they ask the rest of the class their questions.

Reading and writing (WORKBOOK pp.59–60)

5. WB p.59 **Activity 6** Have students complete the crossword puzzle.

Answers

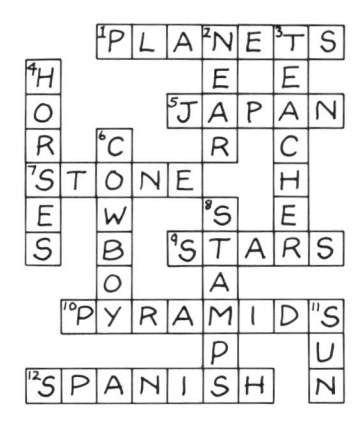

```
 P L A N E T S
 H   E   E
 O   J A P A N
 R C R   C
 S T O N E   H
 E W   S   E
 S B   S T A R S
   O   A
   P Y R A M I D S
   P     U
   S P A N I S H N
```

6. WB p.60 **Activity 7** Pair work: Have students read and follow the instructions to discover a message.

Answers

1   ~~GOOD~~FAKE~~DOG~~
2   BA~~BYE~~RABALL
3   ~~SI~~FROM~~USICE~~
4   ~~ACAT~~CHATTER
5   FU~~BOX~~EGGINS
6   E~~SHAZAM~~FOUR

The message is: *Goodbye from Chatterbox four.*

Ending the lesson

7. Give students a quiz on the stories in the four levels of *American Chatterbox*. The questions can be given to teams of students or individuals. The questions will provide an opportunity to check students' grasp of structures that have been taught through the course.

Questions on Book 1
1. What's the name of Captain Shadow's dog? (Pluto)
2. Who is Zoko? (a robot)
3. Who is Mr. X's friend? (Lifter)
4. Is Mr. X a detective? (No, he isn't. He's a robber.)
5. What does Mr. X have in his basket in the supermarket? (a pizza and a box of chocolate)

Questions on Book 2
6. What is K13? (a dangerous formula)
7. Where does the Professor take Woody and Michael Clacton? (to his island)
8. Does the Professor like ghosts? (No, he doesn't.)
9. In New York, the Professor's friend has a job. What's her job? (She's a waitress.)
10. When do Captain Shadow and the children go to the Professor's apartment? (on Wednesday at twelve o'clock)

Questions on Book 3
11. Does Kate have a cat? (No, she doesn't. She has a parrot.)
12. Did Caroline find a magic stone in Kate's bedroom? (No, she didn't. She found a book of magic and a wand.)
13. What TV program did Ken want to watch? (soccer)
14. Which animal came to Ken, Kate, and Caroline's school? (a chimpanzee)
15. Is swimming Caroline's favorite sport? (No, it isn't. Tennis is her favorite sport.)
16. Why did Uncle John make magic rain at the recreation center? (Because the recreation center building was on fire.)
17. What color is Uncle John's house? (purple)
18. What happened at the zoo? (Spider Smith came on an elephant and stole Uncle John's magic book.)
19. What did Spider Smith do in the museum? (He changed a man into a statue then he changed some bones into a real dinosaur.)
20. Did the dinosaur eat some cars? (No, it didn't. It ate some trees.)
21. Where did Uncle John and the children find the dinosaur? (in the park)
22. Did Uncle John change Spider Smith into a dinosaur? (No, he didn't. He changed Spider Smith into a frog.)
23. How much money did the children get for a reward? ($20,000)
24. What can the Time Machine do? (It can go forward in time to the future and backward to the past.)

Questions on Book 4
25. Where did the children and Uncle John go first in the Time Machine? (to Mars in the future)
26. Why can't robots say the spell to open the box with the Book of Adabra? (Because robots can't talk backward.)
27. Is the Parthenon older than the Book of Adabra? (No, it isn't. The Book of Adabra is older than the Parthenon.)
28. Is Miss Electra the most famous magician in Hollywood? (No, she isn't. Lucky Lorenz is the most famous magician.)
29. Where did uncle John put Ringo Dingo? (in a cage)
30. How many pages did the Queen of Egypt take out of the Book of Adabra? (seven)

Testing

Now is an appropriate time to test students on the previous five units.

These suggestions are intended to complement the reading and writing test exercises contained in the *American Chatterbox* Tests at the end of this Teacher's Book.

- Spelling. Read aloud the following ten words for students to write and spell.

  1. guitar
  2. motorcycle
  3. afraid
  4. alphabet
  5. frightened
  6. necklace
  7. calendar
  8. colorful
  9. everybody
  10. modern

- Dictation. Read aloud each section of the following dictation twice. Have students listen and write.
  The Time Machine arrived in Kate's backyard./ Everybody climbed out./Kate's mom was angry/because the children were late for lunch./ But Spider Smith said a magic spell/and made a wonderful magic lunch.

  Read through the whole dictation again for students to listen and check.

- Composition. Ask students to write five sentences about the picture story on SB p.45: *Jane's music was very loud so ...*, etc.

- Oral assessment. If a test of oral skills is required, use the picture on SB pp.45–46 of the Student Book. Ask students to tell you what happened.

CHATTERBOX TEST BOOK 4

Test 1 (Units 1–5)

♦ **Write sentences about the pictures.** [10 points]

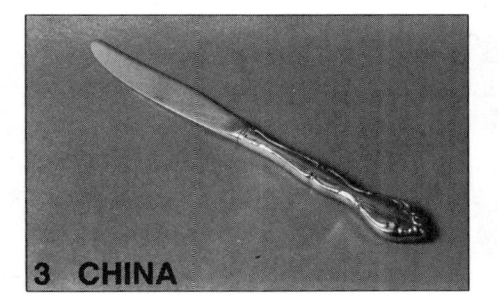

RUSSIA

Example: *This is a Russian bottle. It's made of glass.*

1 **AUSTRALIA**

2 **CANADA**

3 **CHINA**

4 **JAPAN**

5 **AMERICA**

♦ **Write sentences with *must* or *must not* about the pictures.** [5 points]

Example: *You must not stand on the table.*

6. _____ on the bed.

7. _____ in the wastepaper basket.

8. _____ in the classroom.

9. _____ in the storybook.

10. _____

You may make copies of this material for classroom use.

♦ **Write sentences.**   [5 points]

Example: dinosaur/big/house
The dinosaur is bigger than the house.

11. lion/dangerous/dog

12. giraffe/tall/clown

13. ladder/long/snake

14. boy/young/girl

15. book/interesting/movie

♦ **What are their jobs? Write sentences.**   [5 points]

Example: She catches criminals. She works in a police station. *She's a police officer.*

16. She repairs cars. She works in a garage. _____

17. She wears a space suit. She works in a space shuttle. _____

18. He builds houses. He works outside and he carries a ladder. _____

19. He teaches children. He works in a classroom. _____

20. She types letters. She works in an office. _____

[Total: ___ points out of 25]

Test 2 (Units 6–10)

♦ **Look at the pictures. Answer the questions.** [5 points]

Bippo   Zippo   Bonzo

Example: Which clown's nose is the biggest? *Bippo's nose is the biggest.*

1. Which clown's hat is the tallest? _____
2. Which clown's hat is the smallest? _____
3. Which clown's hair is the longest? _____
4. Which clown's mouth is the widest? _____
5. Which clown's box is the heaviest? _____

♦ **Write sentences.** [5 points]

Example: *He'd like to be a mail carrier.*

6. _____
7. _____
8. _____
9. _____
10. _____

♦ **What will they bring to the party? Write sentences.** [5 points]

Example: *She'll bring some bananas.*

11. _____

12. _____

13. _____

14. _____

15. _____

♦ **What are they saying? Complete the sentences. Use *looks like* and *sounds like*.** [10 points]

Example: [Caroline]: *Look! It looks like a door.*

16. [Ken]: Listen! It sounds like _____

17. [Ken]: _____

18. [Ken]: And look! _____

19. [Caroline]: I can hear something. _____

20. [Caroline]: Don't move! _____

[Total: ___ points out of 25]

Test 3 (Units 11–15)

♦ **Write questions and the answers.**   [5 points]

box of tennis balls $5.60
dog $6.00
roller skates $12.00
soccer ball $14.50
skateboard $30.00
kite $4.50

Example:
- What will you buy?
- I'll buy the kite. How much is it?
- It's $4.50.

1. • What will you _____?
   • _____ the skateboard. How _____ is it?
   • It's _____.

2. • What _____?
   • _____ the dog. How _____?
   • _____.

3. • _____
   • _____
   • _____

4. • _____
   • _____
   • _____

5. • _____
   • _____
   • _____

♦ **Read and match.**   [5 points]

Example:

It was a hot day . . .   . . . so I bought a pizza.

6. It wasn't raining . . .   . . . so I put on my coat.

7. The water wasn't cold . . .   . . . so I went to the beach.

8. I was hungry . . .   . . . so I didn't need my umbrella.

9. I was tired . . .   . . . so I went for a swim.

10. It was cold . . .   . . . so I sat on a seat.

♦ **What are they afraid of?** **Complete the sentences.** [5 points]

Example: *Somebody is afraid of ghosts.*

11. Everybody _____

12. Nobody _____

13. Everybody _____

14. Somebody _____

15. Is anybody _____

♦ **Complete the letter.** **Use words from the box.** [10 points]

| made than more bought more so go by plastic will |

Dear Ringo,

I arrived in Japan yesterday. I came here _____ plane because it was faster _____ the boat.

I wanted to buy a present for Kashoki, _____ I went to a big store. In the store there were birds _____ of paper and spiders made of _____. The birds were _____ colorful than the spiders, but the spiders were _____ frightening than the birds. So I _____ a plastic spider.

Tomorrow I'll _____ to Kashoki's house by train. Kashoki was afraid of you, Ringo, but he will like me. I think he _____ tell me about the missing pages from the Book of Adabra. From, Spider

[Total: ___ points out of 25]

WORD LIST

New words list

The number after the word indicates the unit in which students first use the word. Words in the past tense are indicated in bold, words which are not printed in the Student Book are indicated in italic. WB indicates that the word appears in the Workbook. TB indicates that the word appears in the Teacher's Book.

a lot of	11
Aborigine	9
absolutely	10
across	10
actor	8
address (noun)	5
afraid	12
afraid of	14
air	4
album	1
all day	7
alphabet	13
also	11
angrily	9
antelope	7
anything	9
arrived	12
astronaut	2
at first	14
at last	14
attacked	13
Australia	1
be	3
became	8
bedtime	3
bee	8
best	6
better	6
bigger	4
biggest	6
bill (=money)	11

birthday	3
body	3
bought	7
boxes	3
Brazilian	1
Britain	1
British	1
buffalo	7
build (verb)	8
builder	5
by (+ transportation)	13
cabinet	3
calendar	1
Canadian	1
candle	14
cent	11
center	5
child	7
Chinese	1
clapped	12
class	7
cleaner	WB4
cloudy	7
club	5
coin	11
collect (verb)	1
colored	11
colorful	4
continent	9
cook (noun)	5
cotton	12
cowboy	7
crocodile	9
crossroads	14
crunch (verb)	10
dancer	5
dancing	12
dark	3
deer	7
desert	9
did	7
different	2
difficult	2
dime	11
dingo	9

discouraging	7
doctor	5
drank	TB13
dream (noun, verb)	1
dreamed	**1**
dress (noun)	TB1
driver	5
drop (verb)	13
echo (verb)	8
electricity	5
else (= other)	8
England	WB11
English	WB11
enormous	10
European	13
everything	11
exercises	3
experiment (noun)	5
explore (verb)	9
fantastic	6
far	11
farm	5
farmer	5
fast	13
faster	WB4
fastest	6
fatter	WB4
fattest	6
feel	10
feet (pl)	10
fire engine	5
fire fighter	5
fire station	5
fishes (pl)	10
flew	11
float	2
fold (verb)	11
footprint	9
for example	8
forgot	3
for once	8
framed (= incriminated)	8
France	13
French	13

frightened	14
fuel	2
furnish (verb)	8
garage	5
garden	15
get to	10
get (= become)	3
get (= obtain)	3
glass	2
gold	12
good (friend)	5
Good evening	15
got out of	11
gravity	2
Greek	1
guitar	11
gun	7
half	13
happiest	6
harmony	8
heard (past participle)	7
heavier	6
heaviest	6
helmet	2
help (noun)	6
helped	15
hid	12
high	9
hobby	11
hole	9
homemaker	5
horse	6
How much?	11
in the middle of	9
inch	6
Indian	7
invented	13
Italian	11
jaguar	6
Japanese	1

73

WORD LIST

kangaroo	9
keep (= maintain)	10
keep company	8
kids (= children)	5
kilogram	6
knife	10
knock (verb)	9
koala	9
land (noun)	6
lawyer	5
lemon	8
letter (= character)	13
light (opp. dark)	15
like (= similar to)	10
liked	8
line	4
listened	14
live (=exist)	4
longer	4
longest	6
look after	5
lose (verb)	10
love (noun)	8
made of	2
mail carrier	5
mask	6
mat	11
mean (= nasty)	4
meat	12
mechanic	5
met	13
metal	2
mice (pl)	10
mile	4
mine	3
modern	11
more	14
mountain	9
move	2
movie director	10
most (= the majority of)	1
most (superl.)	6
motorcycle	11
mustache	6

must	3
nearer	4
necklace	14
needed	12
nickel (money)	11
night	10
nurse	5
of course	8
office	5
older	4
oldest	6
on the left	14
opened	12
or	11
origami	11
other	2
outback	9
(go) past	7
peace	8
penny	11
perfect	8
perhaps	4
piece	6
place	1
planet	3
plastic	2
pocket	9
popular	8
potato chips	8
pouch	9
pound	6
powder	2
present (= gift)	9
problem (math)	4
program	3
pulled	13
put back	3
put out (= extinguished)	5
quarter (money)	11

queen	1
quicker	9
radio	11
range	7
really	15
record	6
record breaker	6
record player	12
repair	5
rest (= remainder)	14
roam	7
robot	1
rock	9
Roman	13
round (= circular)	11
rules	3
run	6
Russian	1
saddest	6
salesperson	5
sand	9
sat	11
science fiction	8
seat	12
second (time)	6
secretary	5
seldom	7
sell (verb)	5
send out	2
shark	9
sharp	9
sharpest	10
sheep	5
ship	9
shortest	6
shout (verb)	4
shouted	12
showed	15
Shut up!	9
side	11
smaller	4
smallest	6
smile (noun)	10
smiled	12

snowed	13
snow-white	8
so (= consequently)	12
solar system	4
sound (noun)	8
sound (verb)	10
space shuttle	2
space suit	2
Spanish	1
speak	3
special effects	8
stamp (noun)	1
started	12
stories (pl)	3
stupid	9
suitable	10
sunglasses	12
supper	10
sunshine	15
surprise	2
swim (noun)	9
take (train, etc)	9
talked	15
taller	4
tallest	6
tank	2
teach (verb)	8
than	4
their	TB1
thinner	4
thinnest	6
throughout	8
told	4
ton	6
towards	14
toy	11
treasure	9
tree house	TB1
turn left	7
turn off	TB12
turn on	TB12
turtle dove	8
type (verb)	5
type (= sort, kind)	8

WORD LIST

understand	3
unhappy	8
use (verb)	11
useful	3
verb	13
vet	5
waited	12
washed	7
way (= route)	14
Well, well!	10
weigh (verb)	6
What a . . . !	2
wheel	3
whispered	9
wife	12
wild	1
will	9
wives (pl)	12
women (pl)	10
wonderful	5
wool	9
work (verb)	2
would . . . like	8
writing (noun)	13
younger	4
youngest	6
You're welcome	7